TECHNICAL
REPORT

T0302799

Government Consolidation and Economic Development in Allegheny County and the City of Pittsburgh

Rae W. Archibald, Sally Sleeper

Sponsored by the Citizens Advisory Committee on the Efficiency and Effectiveness of City-County Government

RAND

Environment, Energy, and Economic Development

A RAND INFRASTRUCTURE, SAFETY, AND ENVIRONMENT PROGRAM

The research described in this report was sponsored by the Citizens Advisory Committee on the Efficiency and Effectiveness of City-County Government and was conducted under the auspices of the Environment, Energy, and Economic Development program (EEED) within RAND Infrastructure, Safety, and Environment (ISE).

Library of Congress Cataloging-in-Publication Data is available for this publication.

ISBN #978-0-8330-4463-1

The RAND Corporation is a nonprofit research organization providing objective analysis and effective solutions that address the challenges facing the public and private sectors around the world. RAND's publications do not necessarily reflect the opinions of its research clients and sponsors.

RAND® is a registered trademark.

Published 2008 by the RAND Corporation
1776 Main Street, P.O. Box 2138, Santa Monica, CA 90407-2138
1200 South Hayes Street, Arlington, VA 22202-5050
4570 Fifth Avenue, Suite 600, Pittsburgh, PA 15213-2665
RAND URL: http://www.rand.org/
To order RAND documents or to obtain additional information, contact
Distribution Services: Telephone: (310) 451-7002;
Fax: (310) 451-6915; Email: order@rand.org

Preface

This report discusses a relatively narrow topic within the broad framework of metropolitan-area governance: the potential effects of local-government consolidation on a region's economic development. Specifically, the report examines the potential economic-development effects of consolidating Allegheny County and the City of Pittsburgh. Advocates of a metropolitan approach to planning and governance have championed consolidation of local governments for many years. Too many government units spread over too small a geographic area have been seen to be the cause of a long litany of ills, including, for example, urban sprawl, barriers to job growth and business development, and more-expensive-than-necessary government. This report seeks to contribute to understanding the effect of consolidation on future economic development, which is especially critical as Pittsburgh and Allegheny County consider again how their two governments might act to better meet the needs of the region. The Citizens Advisory Committee on the Efficiency and Effectiveness of City-County Government sponsored the research reported here.

Related RAND research is presented in the following documents:

- *A Research Agenda for Assessing the Impact of Fragmented Governance on Southwestern Pennsylvania* (Sleeper, Willis, Rattien, and Lanczos, 2004)
- *Measuring and Understanding Economic Interdependence in Allegheny County* (Sleeper, Willis, Landree, and Grill, 2004)
- *An Economic Development Architecture for New Orleans* (McCarthy, 2008).

The Rand Environment, Energy, and Economic Development Program

This research was conducted under the auspices of the Environment, Energy, and Economic Development Program (EEED) within RAND Infrastructure, Safety, and Environment (ISE). The mission of ISE is to improve the development, operation, use, and protection of society's essential physical assets and natural resources and to enhance the related social assets of safety and security of individuals in transit and in their workplaces and communities. The EEED research portfolio addresses environmental quality and regulation, energy resources and systems, water resources and systems, climate, natural hazards and disasters, and economic development—both domestically and internationally. EEED research is conducted for government, foundations, and the private sector.

Questions or comments about this report should be sent to the project leader, Rae Archibald (Rae_Archibald@rand.org). Information about EEED is available online (http://www. rand.org/ise/environ). Inquiries about EEED projects should be sent to the following address:

Michael Toman, Director
Environment, Energy, and Economic Development Program, ISE
RAND Corporation
1200 South Hayes Street
Arlington, VA 22202-5050
703-413-1100, x5189
Michael_Toman@rand.org

Contents

Tables

Summary

Pittsburgh–Allegheny County: Fragmented and Underachieving

Allegheny County has the dubious distinction of being among the most fragmented counties in the United States in terms of governmental units. It has some 128 municipalities, 101 special districts, and 44 school districts. Looking more widely, the seven-county metropolitan statistical area (MSA) has more than 900 governments, giving the region more governmental units per capita than any other region in the United States.

With such extensive fragmentation, the topic of government consolidation as a way of improving the economic well-being of the area's residents inevitably arises. Aggregate data, when viewed across regions of the country and over time, suggest a positive relationship. As Table S.1 shows, fragmented governance correlates with poor regional performance on population and employment measures. The Pittsburgh MSA, which is the most fragmented of the larger MSAs in the United States, lags even among the six most fragmented MSAs. The Pittsburgh MSA also performed worse than the Commonwealth of Pennsylvania did on these measures.[1] Its population has declined over the past 15 years, and its employment lags the least fragmented MSAs by 16.5 percentage points.

Such disappointing statistics are well known to the leaders of the region. Recently, the mayor of Pittsburgh and the county executive asked the chancellor of the University of

Table S.1
Indicators of Regional Performance, by Degree of Government Fragmentation

Region	Population Change, 1990–2005 (%)	Employment Change, 1990–2005 (%)
Six least fragmented cities	23.7	21.0
Six most fragmented cities	9.8	12.8
Pittsburgh MSA	–3.5	4.5
Pennsylvania	4.4	9.0

SOURCE: U.S. Census Bureau data.

---

[1] Government fragmentation is measured as the number of local governments per 100,000 residents. For this metric, the six least fragmented MSAs are, in order of increasing fragmentation, San Diego (Calif.), Los Angeles–Riverside–Orange County (Calif.), Phoenix-Mesa (Ariz.), Miami–Fort Lauderdale (Fla.), San Francisco–Oakland–San Jose (Calif.), and Tampa–St. Petersburg–Clearwater (Fla.). The six most fragmented cities (also in order of increasing fragmentation) are Cleveland-Akron (Ohio), Kansas City (Mo.-Kan.), Cincinnati (Ohio-Ky.-Ind.), St. Louis (Mo.-Ill.), Minneapolis–St. Paul (Minn.), and Pittsburgh (Pa.) (Orfield, 2002).

Pittsburgh to chair a task force to explore issues surrounding consolidation, whether that might be the provision of joint services or wholesale merger of governments. The task force, in turn, asked RAND to analyze one specific topic that it thought had special import for the region and often was cited as a rationale for consolidation: that consolidation would result in enhanced economic development.

To comply with this request, we reviewed the literature, interviewed experts in the region and across the nation about the relationship between consolidation and economic development, created a framework for analysis, and developed conclusions about the possibilities for enhancing economic development under consolidation.

What Is the Economic-Development Case for Consolidation?

The information we gathered falls naturally into three categories:

- the theoretical case
- the practitioner case
- the academic case.

The Theoretical Case

A review of the theories about consolidation's effects on regional economic development reveals substantive arguments on both sides of the question. Table S.2 summarizes these.

The Practitioner Case

Those directly involved in economic development generally take a more positive view of consolidation's effect on economic development than that found in the theoretical literature. Where consolidation actually has occurred, experts voice opinions that range from mildly positive to enthusiastic. In counties that have not consolidated, we found general support for the idea that consolidation would foster enhanced economic development. That said, those we interviewed were short on specifics of exactly how consolidation did or would do that. But certainly a recurring theme was that unity of leadership, speaking with one voice, and sharing a common vision would have a positive effect on regional economic development.

The Academic Case

Our review of the academic literature suggests that those who have studied consolidation believe that it will enhance a region's *capacity* for economic development and that it *should* help

Table S.2
The Theoretical Case for and Against Consolidation

Arguments for	Arguments Against
Improves technical efficiency	Reduces choice
Reduces fragmented governance	Fails to achieve anticipated economies of scale
Improves regional fiscal and social balance	Spreads urban ills to the suburbs
Enhances economic development	

economic performance. However, we could not find unequivocal evidence that city-county consolidation *does* improve economic development. Neither did we find any strong analysis *refuting* the notion that consolidation can improve it. The empirical work we reviewed does not show statistically significant evidence that consolidation will enhance economic development when measured against a variety of measurements, such as firm or payroll growth. In some cases, statistically significant growth did occur but at the same pace as in the rest of the state or comparable regions, suggesting that the growth might have occurred irrespective of the consolidation.[2] However, the empirical studies are few and the measurement issues difficult, leaving the academic case unsettled.

Expectations of the Impact of Consolidation on Economic Development

The body of material we reviewed does not make an incontrovertible case for the link between consolidation and economic development. Theoretical arguments can be found on either side of the question. Practitioners generally believe that it is helpful but have difficulty pointing to specific connections or results. Academics generally think it should help, but neither the case studies nor the empirical analyses provide strong quantitative support for that feeling. Clearly, we cannot make a definitive, empirical case one way or the other.

In the absence of clear empirical support for the case and divergence among experts, we looked at the body of evidence from many sources. Responses from practitioners suggest an expected effect of consolidation on economic development along specific dimensions that help define a positive case for economic development. When we weigh the body of evidence in total, we conclude that consolidation of the city and county can have a generally positive impact on economic development. We reached this conclusion following a train of logic based on the goals of economic development and the experiences of consolidating entities. First, we identified common goals of economic development. We then reviewed the economic-development process and analyzed some common elements that are indicative of ways in which government can affect that process. We next assessed the evidence relative to a hypothetical consolidation of Pittsburgh and Allegheny County with respect to whether the key elements would flourish or founder in the event of that consolidation.

Based on our assessment of the literature, case studies, and interviews, economic development should include at least three specific goals. One is feeding and sustaining the local economy. This includes such activities as improving schools, reducing crime, and improving infrastructure. It also includes making growth easy for existing businesses and encouraging innovation. A second goal is attracting new businesses and institutions to the region. In this case, unlike the first goal, the focus falls outside the region. The third goal is maintaining or improving the attractiveness of the workforce. Here, actions include capitalizing on the strength of educational institutions and encouraging them to teach the types of skills that are attractive to local employers and those being sought from outside the region.

Building on the evidence, we then identify general characteristics that are frequently cited in support of the proposition that city-county consolidation can improve regional economic development. These key elements of the economic-development case appear in Table S.3, along with more-detailed attributes of each element. The perception of practitioners,

---

[2] Note, however, from Table S.1, that the Pittsburgh MSA lags the state in key indicators.

Table S.3
Salient Elements of an Economic-Development Case

Element	Characteristic
Unity of leadership	One accountable decisionmaker Common vision; speak with one voice Greater regional stature Improved access to state and federal money
Increased planning and development capacity	More-comprehensive planning and coordinated land-use regulation Improved public-private cooperation Larger legal and resource base for attracting and supporting development More-sophisticated economic-development capability
Simpler regulatory procedures for business	Clarity of authority Improved transparency Streamlined permit processing
Reduced intergovernmental competition	Less-fragmented governance Fewer inefficient economic-development subsidies

theorists, and involved citizens with whom we talked, as well as our own analysis, suggest that these elements of consolidation can—and, in some circumstances, do—make a difference in economic performance.

The next step was to consider each of the key elements and its characteristics under two situations: with and without consolidation of the City of Pittsburgh and Allegheny County. Conceptually, we retraced the arguments and assessed where the balance might fall specifically for Pittsburgh–Allegheny County. Table S.4 shows anticipated effects of consolidation on the characteristics based on our assessment of the body of evidence of differences that might show up when comparing an unconsolidated City of Pittsburgh and Allegheny County with a consolidated entity. These assessments are based on the theoretical and empirical literature, case studies, and interviews with practitioners. Our intent is to signal the direction of change, if any, and the intensity that might be expected.

The direction and strength of elements of a possible case for improved economic development through consolidation that we have identified are noncommensurable. We are not proposing that one simply sum the elements that are hypothesized to improve with consolidation and declare the case to have been made. The assessments are distillations of arguments found in the literature, case studies, and interviews with practitioners and experts. The direction of a change is based on the body of evidence; however, the magnitude of the impact is our subjective judgment based on the same evidence. Any number of weighting schemes could be applied that would change a naïve interpretation of the number of elements hypothesized to improve under consolidation. But for us, calling out some elements of a case and setting forth subjective magnitudes of a change is a way of sharpening the debate and squeezing the empirical evidence and subjective inferences into metrics through which informed citizens can agree or disagree about the effects of some factor, thereby improving their discourse on future public policy.

Two overarching points emerge from the assessments reflected in Table S.4. First, consolidation can improve economic development. Even though, in some cases, consolidation of the city and county may have little or no effect on a given characteristic of economic development, we judge that seven of the characteristics improve under consolidation, some substantially. The

Table S.4
Elements of an Economic-Development Case and Anticipated Effects from the Consolidation of the City of Pittsburgh and Allegheny County

Element	Characteristic	Anticipated Effect of Consolidation on Characteristic
Unity of leadership	One accountable decisionmaker	Greatly improve
	Common vision; speak with one voice	Greatly improve
	Greater regional stature	No change
	Improved access to state and federal money	Likely no change
Increased planning and development capacity	More-comprehensive planning and coordinated land-use regulation	Improve
	Improved public-private cooperation	No change
	Larger legal and resource base for attracting and supporting development	Improve
	More-sophisticated economic-development capability	Little or no change
Simpler regulatory procedures for business	Clarity of authority	Improve
	Improved transparency	Improve
	Streamlined permit processing	Little or no change
Reduced intergovernmental competition	Less-fragmented governance	Improve
	Fewer inefficient economic-development subsidies	No change

second key observation is that unity of leadership is affected to the greatest extent. Accountability and a common vision weigh heavily for consolidation, and we conclude that this dimension alone of the case for consolidation holds promise for improving economic development.

Conclusions

The varied nature of consolidations and the difficulties of measuring improvement in economic development with or without consolidation make it impossible to find definitive evidence one way or the other that consolidating the City of Pittsburgh and Allegheny County should improve economic development. But neither does the evidence suggest that consolidation would have a negative effect on economic development.

Even if not demonstrable empirically in other settings, key signs point to some version of consolidation as being helpful for the City of Pittsburgh and Allegheny County. First, *improved policy direction and unity of leadership seems within grasp, and our judgment is that this can have a positive—albeit difficult to measure—effect on economic development.* Second, *improved coordination and sharpening of economic-development initiatives seem within reach, and our judgment is that this would have a positive (although, again, likely to be difficult to measure) effect on economic development.*

These conclusions come with caveats. First, any such economic-development gains will require *enhanced coordination and collaboration with the private sector.* The consolidated entity still will have to deal with the need to rationalize the myriad of economic-development efforts under way within the region, including the worthy public-private partnerships and the perception of a bewildering number of programs and agencies that seem to have some responsibility for the economic well-being of the region. Second, *fragmented regulatory processes and intergovernmental competition will remain drags on regional economic development* if the consolidation scheme involves only the city and county. Finally, we recognize the inherent limitations of employing a body-of-evidence approach, described earlier. The direction and magnitude of effects are our judgments based on distillations from our research and interviews. However, the process can sharpen the debate about consolidation and provide a common framework for discussion.

Acknowledgments

As might be expected in a report in which important sources of information are individuals who agree to spend their precious time being interviewed, we first and foremost are indebted to those who talked with us and so freely shared their wealth of information and considerable insights across a wide range of topics related to governmental consolidation and economic development. Although any errors of interpretation are, of course, ours, we found an informed and dedicated set of academics and practitioners who are working the vineyard of economic development.

We wish to thank the Citizens Advisory Committee on the Efficiency and Effectiveness of City-County Government, chaired by University of Pittsburgh chancellor Mark Nordenberg, for sponsoring this research. Special thanks go to vice chancellor G. Reynolds Clark for his timely feedback and support.

Our RAND colleagues Amy Maletic and Jake Dembosky provided valuable assistance throughout, and we thank them. We also recognize the efforts of Victoria Wiedrich, executive assistant, and Jennifer Gelman, RAND librarian, for their significant contributions. Special thanks go to Jerry Sollinger, our colleague who specializes in transforming the musings of researchers, putting them into reports that make structural sense with understandable prose. Jerry's ability to work quickly and under time pressure is remarkable. We thank the director of the RAND Pittsburgh office, Barry Balmat, for his feedback and guidance through this study.

As with any analytical work, the criticism and helpful comments of colleagues are a key ingredient to developing a better product. We greatly appreciate the comments from our reviewers, Henry Willis of RAND and Jerry Paytas, director of research at GSP Consulting. Their insights greatly improved our report. Finally, we appreciate the hard work and careful eyes of our support staff, Megan McKeever, Christopher Dirks, and our perceptive and timely editor, Lisa Bernard.

Abbreviations

EEED	Environment, Energy, and Economic Development Program
ISE	RAND Infrastructure, Safety, and Environment
MSA	metropolitan statistical area
NACo	National Association of Counties
RAD	Allegheny Regional Asset District
SPC	Southwestern Pennsylvania Commission

CHAPTER ONE

Introduction

Background

Pittsburgh and Allegheny County are among the most highly fragmented regions in the country, with some 128 municipalities, 101 special districts, and 44 school districts in Allegheny County alone. There are more than 900 governmental units in the seven-county metropolitan statistical area (MSA), giving the region more governments per capita than any other major region in the United States.[1] Thus it is not surprising that this periodically leads to public debate about the wisdom of combining local governments in the region. Allegheny County adopted a home-rule charter in 1998 that created a county council and an elected county executive and permitted municipalities within the county to dissolve voluntarily (although none has yet done so). The City of Pittsburgh has faced severe financial stress in the past several years, leading to special state legislation and enhanced financial oversight.

Whether fragmentation imposes a financial penalty in terms of lost jobs and businesses often provokes debate. Those arguing that it does not (and that it may even foster growth) often cite anecdotal evidence of job gains in one sector or another as evidence. However, the empirical data are less ambiguous. Table 1.1 captures indicators of regional performance with respect to changes in employment as a function of the level of fragmentation. The table compares the least fragmented cities, the most fragmented, Pittsburgh MSA, and Pennsylvania, showing the population change and the employment change for a 15-year period. The data show that, during the period, population in Pittsburgh actually declined, while that of the state rose. Furthermore, at a 4.5-percent change, job growth was relatively anemic, lagging the state by 4.5 percentage points, other fragmented cities by 8.3 percentage points, and the least fragmented cities by nearly 16.5 percentage points.

The difficulty of effective governance with so many entities involved and the possible economic benefits that might accrue from a more streamlined organization have led to considerations of various consolidations over time. Recently, the county executive and the mayor of Pittsburgh again signaled that some increased cooperation, collaboration, or merger of the governments of the city and county should be explored. They asked University of Pittsburgh chancellor Mark Nordenberg to recruit and chair a task force of knowledgeable, involved citizens and officials who would explore in depth the issues surrounding consolidation—whether that might be defined as joint provision of some services or wholesale merger of governments.

---

[1] See, for example, the work of Christopher Briem, University Center for Social and Urban Research, University of Pittsburgh, and Harold D. Miller, president of Future Strategies LLC and adjunct professor at Carnegie Mellon University Heinz School of Public Policy and Management, often reported in Miller (undated), for extensive presentation and analysis of data regarding the Pittsburgh region.

Table 1.1
Indicators of Regional Performance, by Degree of Government Fragmentation

Region	Population Change, 1990–2005 (%)	Employment Change, 1990–2005 (%)
Six least fragmented cities	23.7	21.0
Six most fragmented cities	9.8	12.8
Pittsburgh MSA	–3.5	4.5
Pennsylvania	4.4	9.0

SOURCE: U.S. Census Bureau.

NOTE: Government fragmentation is measured as the number of local governments per 100,000 residents. For this metric, the six least fragmented MSA cities are, in order or increasing fragmentation, San Diego (Calif.), Los Angeles–Riverside–Orange County (Calif.), Phoenix-Mesa (Ariz.), Miami–Fort Lauderdale (Fla.), San Francisco–Oakland–San Jose (Calif.), and Tampa–St. Petersburgh–Clearwater (Fla.). The six most fragmented cities (also in order of increasing fragmentation) are Cleveland-Akron (Ohio), Kansas City (Mo.-Kan.), Cincinnati (Ohio-Ky.-Ind.), St. Louis (Mo.-Ill.), Minneapolis–St. Paul (Minn.), and Pittsburgh (Pa.) (Orfield, 2002).

The Citizens Advisory Committee on the Efficiency and Effectiveness of County-City Government, as the task force was named, working with local experts, community leaders, and leaders from other regions involved in consolidation, has been exploring the full range of issues that arise from consolidation and the arguments for and against various forms of consolidation.

The committee's exploration revealed that one specific hypothesis—consolidation can enhance economic development—had special relevance for the Pittsburgh region and often was cited as an important benefit of consolidation. So, among the myriad of other benefits and costs of consolidation that the committee members were exploring, they asked RAND to contribute to their deliberations by providing information and analysis on this one specific topic.

The RAND Study and How We Went About It

Study Focus

Consistent with the committee's request, we focused on the topic of assessing whether the consolidation of Allegheny County and the City of Pittsburgh could lead to improved economic development of the region. It is important to note what this report is not. This report is not about consolidation in general. Many issues besides economic development are important when considering consolidation. And, as we say as our report unfolds, consolidation has many meanings and versions. We view our report as one put into the committee's deliberations; it has a task far greater than the scope of this report.

Study Approach

We used a multidimensional, body-of-evidence approach to understand the potential effects on regional economic development of consolidating the City of Pittsburgh and Allegheny County. We examined findings and evidence in literature and case studies to explore the empirical evidence of a relationship in other settings; we interviewed economic professionals and practitioners in 13 regions, both consolidated and unconsolidated, to collect first-hand information on the relationship; we interviewed academics who have studied this area; and we interviewed local individuals to obtain information on, among other things, regional barriers to economic development. Using these resources, we developed a framework to evaluate the potential effect of consolidation on economic health in the city and county. Next, we briefly describe the literature search, interviews, and analytic approach.

Review of Literature. We reviewed an extensive range of empirical and theoretical literature related to our study question. We reviewed empirical studies that tested the relationship between structural government consolidation and various theoretical constructs, including its relationship to economic performance. Only a small number of authors have conducted research on the particular question of interest, though there is a vast literature on regionalism more broadly defined. The empirical studies that directly relate to our topic provide frameworks for analysis, insight into data availability, and limitations in measuring changes brought about by consolidation. The metropolitan economy and general governance literature, while not always directly related to our question, also was useful. The literature places consolidation itself into perspective as one of many possibilities in a range of functional and structural changes and places city and county consolidation in the broader framework of metropolitan governance.

Also included in the literature review are case studies of regions that have consolidated, as well as those that have attempted consolidation but failed at the ballot box. The case studies are not empirical tests of the effect of consolidation on a particular region, though many are careful analyses that follow a consistent case-study methodology. They provide the context and background leading to the decision to pursue some form of structural consolidation; the efforts that preceded a change; characteristics of a region that are not easily captured by demographic, census, or labor statistics; and perceptions (and some evidence) about changes subsequent to a consolidation. Finally, we examined literature on economic growth and development not directly related to consolidation, to obtain the most-current thoughts on measures and metrics of a local economy and the characteristics of a healthy economy.

Interviews. We conducted structured interviews with economic-development professionals and practitioners in 13 regions around the United States. The regions were selected based a review of the literature and discussions with academic and economic-development professionals. We selected a mix of consolidated and unconsolidated city and county entities (five consolidated and eight unconsolidated, of which six attempted consolidation but failed). We included some regions that were considered competitors to Pittsburgh and Allegheny County and some that shared demographic and historical similarities. We developed a structured interview protocol (see the appendix) to gather information on measures of economic vitality, aids and barriers to economic success, the effect of that region's governance on its own performance, competitors with the region, and specific questions about the importance of leadership and streamlined management of the economic function to its own regional performance. We interviewed multiple professionals within a region whenever possible, for a total of 22 individual interviews.

Using a set of questions similar to those contained in the appendix, we also conducted interviews with academics specializing in our area of interest and with economic-development professionals and practitioners in southwestern Pennsylvania. Interviews with academics focused on empirical evidence to support or refute relationships between economic growth and consolidation, theoretical arguments that may help explain results, and requests for additional material that might have been missed in our searches. Interviews with local professionals covered the same set of questions as the (nonlocal) regional and academic interviews but focused more specifically on interviewee experiences in the southwestern Pennsylvania region. These professionals were asked to provide answers based on (1) their experience within the region; (2) experiences prior to their current position or to locating in the region, where applicable; and (3) a thought experiment about the effect of consolidating Pittsburgh and Allegheny County on aiding or preventing economic development for each entity and the region as a whole.

Analytic Approach

We examined the literature to find empirical evidence supporting or refuting our research question. No smoking gun provides definitive proof, yet there is suggestive evidence.[2] We synthesized the literature reviews and case studies to obtain the core arguments related to our primary research questions as well as to understand the broader issues associated with consolidation that may affect economic performance, albeit indirectly. Our interviews do not provide *statistical* evidence; we use the interviews to provide support for (or against) the arguments in the literature. We used the evidence from literature and interviews to develop a framework to assess the likelihood of achieving changes in economic development in Pittsburgh and Allegheny County. This framework consists of comparing a (hypothetical) consolidated city and county government and the existing structure against a series of factors that contribute to a healthy economy. The limitation of this approach is immediately apparent—namely, we cannot directly compare the two forms of governance against traditional measures of economic development, such as the growth of new jobs in a region.

How This Report Is Organized

The remainder of this report is organized in the following way. Chapter Two describes the history of city-county consolidations in the United States, including the types and some of the impetus for consolidation. It then goes on to describe the theoretical reasons for consolidating or not consolidating. Chapter Three describes the views of those who have participated in consolidations and the academics who have studied this issue. Chapter Four focuses on the main issue of this report: economic development. It discusses the goals, how to measure them, and the elements of an economic-development case. Chapter Five builds on the material in Chapter Four by applying it to the specific case of consolidating the City of Pittsburgh and Allegheny County. Finally, Chapter Six presents our conclusions.

---

[2]   As discussed in succeeding sections, there is ample *theoretical* support that structural consolidation should be positively related to economic performance. The lack of *statistically* valid evidence has frustrated researchers. Reasons for its absence include that (1) the limited number of consolidations to date have been in communities of vastly different size and different forms, making comparisons difficult; (2) "true" consolidation apparently has never occurred, since most successful consolidations have strayed from a complete convergence of governments to satisfy a wide range of perceived opposition arguments; (3) the use of "jobs" in various forms as the measure of regional improvement, while politically desirable and easily defined, may not be the best measure of regional improvement; and (4) there are no easy control groups or comparative regions or areas with which to compare economic performance before and after consolidation.

CHAPTER TWO

City-County Consolidations: History and Theoretical Rationales

This chapter briefly reviews the history of city-county consolidations. It also presents the theoretical arguments—pro and con—for such consolidations.

History

City-county consolidations are, in a statistical sense, rare. And they are quite different events—so different that one observer has called *city-county consolidation* a misnomer. There have been 37 city-county consolidations in the United States, starting with New Orleans, Louisiana, in 1805 and ending (so far) with Georgetown–Quitman County, Georgia, in 2006 (NACo, undated). This is from a universe of more than 3,000 counties in the United States. Table 2.1 shows the 10 successful consolidations from 1990 through 2006. All these consolidations—except for the boroughs in Alaska and the Kansas City–Wyandotte County, Kansas consolidation—were in the southern part of the United States, and only one involved a county population of more than 500,000. According to the National Association of Counties (NACo), there have been at least 31 failed attempts to consolidate during the same period. Des Moines, Iowa, and Albuquerque, New Mexico, failed twice during that period. The preponderance of

Table 2.1
Successful City-County Consolidations Since 1990

Location	Year Consolidated	2006 Population
Athens–Clarke County, Ga.	1990	113,000
Lafayette–Lafayette Parish, La.	1992	203,000
City and Borough of Yukatat, Alaska	1992	700
Augusta–Richmond County, Ga.	1995	193,000
Kansas City–Wyandotte County, Kan.	1997	156,000
Louisville–Jefferson County, Ky.	2000	702,000
Hartsville–Trousdale County, Tenn.	2000	8,000
City and Borough of Haines, Alaska	2002	2,200
Cusseta–Chattahoochee County, Ga.	2003	14,000
Georgetown–Quitman County, Ga.	2006	2,500

SOURCES: Consolidation dates from NACo (undated). Population data from U.S. Census Bureau (undated).

those failed consolidation attempts also were in the southern United States or Alaska, with the notable exceptions of Spokane, Washington; Sacramento, California; Des Moines, Iowa; and Albuquerque, New Mexico.

Most of the consolidations have involved relatively small populations. As shown in Table 2.2, only four consolidations since 1960 involved counties with a population of more than 500,000. Allegheny County has a population of about 1.2 million people, and the City of Pittsburgh has a population of about 345,000. The Pittsburgh MSA has a population of about 2.3 million. Based on size and region, these consolidations are not easily matched with a possible consolidation of Pittsburgh and Allegheny County.

But the story is more complicated than this. Political scientists distinguish between *structural* consolidation (in which the services provided, the governance bodies, and the geography of the area become one, or close to one, with school districts, for example, often being excluded), and *functional* consolidation (in which many or most services provided and boundaries are consolidated, but other service institutions and boundaries remain). The remaining units could be local governments, special districts (for example, water treatment or other regional services), school districts, or other special-purpose, quasigovernmental agencies.

Virtually all the modern-day consolidations have been functional ones, each with a different set of taxing, service provision, and governance outcomes. Complete consolidations are extremely rare. We could not find any complete consolidations, at least of a size with potential relevance to Pittsburgh–Allegheny County. Thus, although city-county consolidations are tracked and counted as similar events, they really are a continuum of events, some modestly similar and some truly dissimilar.

Usually, there is a history preceding consolidation of some kind of shared service arrangements, for example, providing for common water treatment, sewage treatment, tax collection, or emergency-service dispatching. Usually, there is also a history of failure at the ballot box. That is, voters have turned down one or more measures to consolidate before a successful consolidation measure was passed. Because of this, the measures that do pass frequently include compromises that may represent less than full consolidation but are intended to overcome perceived reasons for earlier failure. (See, for example, the case studies in Leland and Thurmaier, 2004.)

Typically, school districts and some other special-purpose districts (e.g., water treatment, mosquito abatement, flood protection, power) are not absorbed into the consolidated entity. In some cases, complete municipalities within the county other than the one or more actually

Table 2.2
City-County Consolidations Since 1960 with Populations of More Than 500,000

Location	Year Consolidated	2006 Population	
		County	Metropolitan Area
Nashville–Davidson County, Tenn.	1962	549,000	1,120,000
Jacksonville–Duval County, Fla.	1967	782,000	1,000,000
Indianapolis–Marion County, Ind.	1969	784,000	1,500,000
Louisville–Jefferson County, Ky.	2000	702,000	992,000

SOURCES: Consolidation dates from NACo (undated). Population data from U.S. Census Bureau (undated).

consolidated are left out. Often, there is unincorporated geographic area absorbed into the new government, not unlike the annexation process. In some cases, tax-sharing arrangements that existed before consolidation remain afterward, subject to whatever guidelines and geographical boundaries were in place before consolidation.

State governments have quite different laws regulating what types of consolidation are allowed and the parameters of elections that must take place to effect a consolidation. Not infrequently, localities have had to seek state legislation to enable the particular consolidation envisioned. Finally, as noted earlier, almost all consolidations include overlay governmental or quasigovernmental units. Examples of these include the metropolitan planning organizations that the federal government mandates be set up in order to receive certain types of federal funding (in the case of the greater Pittsburgh region, the Southwestern Pennsylvania Commission [SPC]), multicounty planning or economic-development organizations, and all manner of other special-purpose districts.

In short, in discussing city-county consolidation, the conversation involves events with as many—if not more—dissimilarities than similarities.

City-County Consolidation in the Context of Reform

City-county consolidations are part of the history of good-government reforms begun in the early 20th century. Reacting to the political machines running many cities, reformers touted professional management and the assumed consequent efficiency that would bring to cities among many types of reform. Leland and Johnson (2004) placed consolidation in the context of a wide set of reforms, including (1) centralizing authority and placing it in the hands of professional managers, (2) shrinking the long ballot to require fewer elected officials (for example, eliminating voting for such offices as the coroner or the registrar of deeds), (3) creating metropolitan forms of government, (4) introducing at-large elected local officials in addition to officials elected by districts, (5) introducing nonpartisan local elections, (6) introducing merit-based pay, (7) trying to introduce scientific expertise and expert knowledge as a basis for local government decisionmaking, and (8) touting the council-manager form of government as the ideal.

Of course, not all cities or counties adopted all these reforms over the course of the 20th century, and some larger and older cities resisted many of them. Recently, the City of San Diego (Calif.) voted for a so-called strong mayor form of government to replace its council-manager form of government, in what early reformers would see as a backward step. However, a key argument for that change was that improved unity of leadership (one point of accountability) would lead to better government. This is an argument for city-county consolidation that is heard frequently and helps place city-county consolidations in the long history of attempts to improve local government and, by implication, a community's quality of life. We now turn to the theoretical arguments for and against consolidation.

Theoretical Arguments for Consolidation

The theoretical case for consolidation is advanced on many fronts, including arguments that consolidation can improve efficiency in the delivery of services, eliminate fragmented governance, and improve fiscal and social balance. The efficiency argument suggests the achievement of economies of scale and the elimination of duplication of services, thereby lowering costs. The less-fragmented governance argument suggests improved coordination among governmental units, improved capacity to deliver services through a more professionalized bureaucracy, enhanced planning capability, and, importantly, unity of leadership. The fiscal- and social-balance arguments suggest increased citizen participation, more-equitable tax and service burdens, and, importantly, enhanced economic development.[1]

Improving Technical Efficiency

The promise of efficiency rests on plausible grounds. Consolidated governments are assumed to achieve economies of scale in the delivery of services, with the end result expected to be lowered costs of government as average costs are spread across more users. But, for a panoply of reasons, including legacy costs (notably pension obligations), noncompatible salary and wage schedules, elusive scale economies in the delivery of labor-intensive and neighborhood services, increased transaction costs for the operation of large governments, and increased appetites for more or higher-quality services, the lower costs that this theory suggests seem not to have been realized in most instances. Notably, studies on technical efficiency have not been able to control for the quality of the service or product being delivered, a deficiency that must be overcome for analysts to make a convincing case. Richard Feiock—one of the few academics who has studied consolidations carefully—concluded,

> The progressives promised cost savings through economies of scale, reduced duplication of effort, and greater technical capacity in service provision. These arguments have been largely debunked by empirical research in the last fifteen years. (Carr and Feiock, 2004, p. 44)

Reducing Fragmented Governance

A strong theoretical case can be made that consolidation reduces fragmented governance just from the fact that some externalities (third-party benefits or costs not borne by the producers or consumers of specific goods or services) existing before consolidation are internalized by the combined government. With the stroke of a consolidation pen, the previous third parties are now inside the same governance purview. At least theoretically, these interdependencies that were previously resolved (if at all) by two or more separate governmental units or the courts, for example, are funneled up to only one instead of several executive decisionmakers (remembering, however, that all city-county consolidations have retained an elected policy and legislative body, sometimes with more rather than fewer members than before).

By the same token, there also is a plausible argument that consolidation improves coordination between or among the governments consolidated. For example, previous departments that may have been at odds because they served different masters in different local governments will have to resolve their differences under one master—one that presumably does not present conflicting priorities. Policies that may have been conflicting, overlapping, or internally inconsistent when two or more governments were prosecuting separate approaches may have a greater chance of being reconciled under a combined government.

Consolidation plausibly brings improved technical capacity to deliver services as the size of government increases and the demands require a more skilled bureaucracy (Felbinger, 1984; Frisken, 1997). A small township of a few thousand people is unlikely to attract or have the

---

[1] See, among others, Feiock and Carr (1997), Carr and Feiock (2002, 2004), and Leland and Thurmaier (2005).

resources to pay for the most skilled and experienced staff compared to large municipalities. (See Lembeck, Kelsey, and Fasic, 2001, for example.) Setting aside the issue of cost, consolidation is expected to bring increased *capacity* to serve, including increased legal power to attract businesses (Feiock and Carr, 1997). The crucial inference is whether that increased capacity can deliver a better outcome for the consolidated entity as a whole.

Many observers note that consolidation should bring enhanced planning capability (see, for example, Feiock and Carr, 1997). Competition between or among the consolidated entities should subside dramatically, although it is unlikely to vanish, as narrow interests are merged into a larger metropolitan planning approach. Land-use regulations can be rationalized and adjudicated over a larger geographic region and can include functions that arguably should be planned on a larger scale. Transportation is an obvious example, as are sewerage, water treatment, and flood control. But another payoff for economic development comes from the potential to focus the land-use planning process and streamline implementation to make it easier for firms to locate, relocate, and grow in a region. Reducing the number of governmental units and the number of regulatory schemes with which a firm has to deal to move into the area or to accomplish indigenous growth has popular intuitive appeal.

Finally, within the general rubric of eliminating fragmented governance is the argument that a consolidated government can speak with one voice and sharpen the accountability of senior decisionmakers. This unity-of-leadership argument is intriguing because it embraces a principle that cuts two ways. On the one hand, eliminating, say, a mayor and a county executive in favor of one metro executive does hold the promise of streamlining and focusing decisionmaking over a larger population and greater geographic area. On the other hand, such focusing increases the power of the metro executive, concentrating it in a way that could give rise to the specter of the so-called strong mayors and their political machines that caused the early–20th-century reformers to preach good government in the first place.

Nevertheless, as we discuss in the next section, one of the strongest arguments for consolidation in the literature and that we heard during our interviews was that the positive effects from unity of leadership are unmistakable and can be profound.

Improving Regional Fiscal and Social Balance

There is a stream of support for consolidation on the basis of increased citizen participation and democracy. The argument suggests that greater government accountability rewards participation, begetting more participation. It also suggests that smaller, parochial interests become subject to the light of day, providing a more democratic discourse and, potentially, more-equitable outcomes. Also, the argument suggests that fragmentation effectively keeps large, important regional issues, such as sprawl and regional economic development, from being acted on in a comprehensive, coordinated fashion.[2]

Another theoretical argument for consolidation has been that it can reduce fiscal and social inequalities, especially those perceived between urban central cities and their suburbs. The voluminous metropolitan government and planning literature is filled with pleas for a regional approach to governance—pleas arguing that many local governments acting independently cannot solve the problems that cities, suburbs, and edge cities face. According to the

---

[2] Feulner, Hautier, and Walsh (2005) cited a number of references on this point, ranging from early work by Dahl (1967) to more-recent work by Drier, Mollenkopf, and Swanstrom (2001). See also Kugler and Bula (1999) for a discussion of fragmentation's effects on citizen participation in government.

theory, there are too many externalities and resulting inequalities, there is too much counter-productive competition among communities, and the visions for the future are too narrow and too piecemeal to build and sustain a healthy economy. Consolidation is one of the prescribed cures for these ills, although, in reality, few consolidations tackle fiscal and social disparities head on. Carve-outs for exiting taxing and service-delivery agreements and for local governments not being consolidated are frequent, as we have already noted, and minority interests of all sorts frequently are protected in one way or another in the final consolidation charters that make it past voters or legislatures.

Nevertheless, consolidation, in theory, certainly does open up the possibility for redressing various kinds of inequalities—for example, in the delivery of services or in taxing for public services and undeniable externalities, such as pollution control or transportation infrastructure.

We come now to the last argument for consolidation under the category of improving fiscal and social health and that is the primary focus of this report: enhanced economic development. Although there have been no large city-county consolidations since Louisville–Jefferson County (Ky.) in 2000 (which took full effect in 2003), several communities continue to debate the possibility of some kind of consolidation. Scholars who have studied the prior successes and failures of consolidation efforts and monitor and advise ongoing discussions have concluded that enhanced economic development has become the favored reason used to promote contemporary city-county consolidation (Leland and Thurmaier, 2005; Carr and Feiock, 2002; Carr, Bae, and Lu, 2006). We address these issues more fully in succeeding chapters.

Theoretical Arguments Against Consolidation

Most of the arguments against consolidation end up being location- and circumstance-specific, since there is such great variation in the communities and the plans for consolidation. This leads to a highly eclectic list of potential opposing arguments. However, we have found it useful to highlight three of the more generic points, each of which is manifested in different ways in different communities: (1) fragmentation to a certain extent is good, and consolidation unduly restricts citizens' choices to live in an area that provides the bundles of goods and services that meet their preferences; (2) diseconomies of scale rather than economies of scale will accompany consolidation; and (3) consolidation will bring all of the problems of the central city—especially fiscal burdens—to its surroundings, without concomitant benefits. These arguments will sound familiar, since they tend to be mirror images of the arguments for consolidation discussed previously. We address these in turn.

Loss of Choice
Public-choice theorists describe a world in which citizens shop around for a bundle of goods and services, then choose to locate in the community that best meets their preferences for the services, quality, and price. Too much consolidation hinders this process by restricting broad consumer choice. Charles Tiebout (1956) proposed this idea, but many scholars have advanced versions of it since then.[3] Competition among local governments is good, the theorist argue, since the local governments will compete to provide equivalent bundles of services at lower cost or will select different bundles of services along a continuum of service level, quality, and price,

---

[3]   For a review of the history of this approach, see Howell-Moroney (2008).

thus providing—in the long run—a more efficient region overall in fulfilling citizen preferences. This achieves so-called allocative efficiency, in economists' jargon. If the local government cannot produce the services efficiently itself, it will contract with other local governments
or with the private sector to do so.

The political-science version of this economic argument suggests that, because of competition, local government officials will pay closer attention to their constituents' needs, thus
allowing for more democratic participation in local government. The need to be responsive
forces local politicians to encourage participation and to make access to government decisions
as easy and transparent as possible. Consolidation breaks that connection, or at least attenuates it.

This thesis is strongest when there are few externalities to be adjudicated. The point of
the regional-planning theorists that some bundles of service (e.g., transportation) cannot be
provided as effectively in a competitive, fragmented, local-government world as in a more consolidated world highlights the mirror imaging of the arguments for and against consolidation.
On the one hand, one should have choice, and we will have better choices if there are many
jurisdictions competing to provide us with the best community in which to live based on our
preferences. With our neighbors, we will be close to our government and have a clear path to
our elected officials. On the other hand, if the very real externalities of that fragmentation
cannot be solved (in economic terms, by having the winners somehow pay off the losers), we
will be worse off than we would be otherwise, by breathing polluted air that someone else sent
our way, by being late for work because we have to travel through a jurisdiction disinclined to
pay for widening a thoroughfare, or by finding ourselves living in the shadow of a tall building that the neighboring jurisdiction chose not to regulate, for example. Although most all
citizens appear to grumble—sometimes vociferously—about the externalities with which they
live, many, if not most, also show strong support for keeping as much local control as possible.
Thus, as theoretical as the public-choice argument against consolidation may be, it is a formidable one. In the words of more than one of the people with whom we spoke for this report,
"Yes, think regionally, but *act* locally."

Failure to Achieve Anticipated Economies of Scale

This argument has several parts. Transaction costs (for example, increased coordination
requirements) will increase with consolidation, driving up service-provision costs or at least
not reducing them, and citizens' transaction costs will be increased as citizens grapple with a
larger, more bureaucratic government.

Chris Pineda, in a short piece for the Ash Institute for Democratic Governance and
Innovation at Harvard University, nicely outlines five causes of diseconomies of scale (Pineda,
2005). First, scale economies in labor-intensive services are much harder to achieve than they
are in capital-intensive services. For example, doubling the number of garbage-collection customers may not provide for a reduction in the number of garbage collectors per customer that
existed prior to consolidation. If the service was right-sized to start with (including capital
equipment and relative pay scales) in each locality prior to consolidation, then some new tech-
nology or change in service levels likely will be needed to achieve economies of scale.

Second, consolidation may distance the bureaucrats from their customers' day-to-day
needs. The larger enterprise has increased needs for coordination (think middle managers), and
senior managers have intermediaries between them and the final customer. This puts them out
of touch and less responsive than senior managers would be in the nonconsolidated setting.

Observers have argued that the citizens in consolidated governments will sustain a loss of intimacy with their local government, leading to less accountability. Notice that this is the mirror image of the argument that suggests that consolidation can bring better accountability. The two arguments are not wholly incompatible, however, since consolidation may indeed bring greater policy coherence and direction from the top but still not be able to deliver the envisioned outcomes on the ground.

Third, merged personnel systems seem to result in personnel-related costs rising to the highest level of the preexisting structure, and, usually, there are legacy costs (such as pension obligations) and sometimes job security for existing employees. These realities also hinder the chances of achieving economies of scale. Similarly, fourth, merged systems may lead to quality creep in the delivery of services when the consolidated entity ends up standardizing service to the highest preexisting levels. These levels usually entail higher costs, thereby raising the average costs across the consolidated system.

Finally, fifth, the amortization of one-time transition costs may be nontrivial, again hindering cost savings and even leading to diseconomies. Merging or upgrading various computer systems to handle new customers and new volumes are examples of transition costs that can drag down even savings envisioned in the longer term. As pointed out earlier, the empirical literature on technical-efficiency effects tends to support the conclusion that cost savings from consolidation are likely to be minimal or nonexistent, even accounting for measurement difficulties that may not adequately capture benefits. That is one reason that the economic-development argument has come to the fore in recent years.

Consolidation Will Spread the Burdens of the Central City to the Suburbs

The long history of failed consolidation attempts demonstrates the suspicions and fears of consolidation by citizens inside but also, frequently, outside the central city. Sometimes, those inside the central city are concerned about maintaining adequate representation in a consolidation, fearing that consolidation is a device to diminish minority representation. This is a legitimate concern that proponents of consolidation have tried to address one way or another in the latest consolidation attempts. (See, for example, Savitch and Vogel, 2004.)

However, it is frequently the fears and suspicions of citizens outside the central city that must be overcome for consolidation to be approved at the ballot box. These fears range from increased social burdens to increased tax burdens and often involve sensitive, or hot-button, political issues that simmer just beneath the surface of general political discourse. The specter of moving more social welfare agencies or services into the suburbs or introducing more low- and moderate-income housing into suburban areas looms large in arguments against consolidation. Similarly, but perhaps not as emotionally, opponents see consolidation as simply another way to move central-city fiscal burdens out to the suburbs. In short, the argument goes, under consolidation, taxes for non–central-city residents will rise more than they would have without consolidation.

The Pittsburgh region already has a version of this, one that arguably has made regional assets better off and added some stability to local government funding, but one that still raises concerns from suburban taxpayers.[4] Advocates on the other side of the argument suggest that

---

[4] The Allegheny Regional Asset District (RAD) was created in 1994 to manage an imposed 1-percent countywide sales tax. The purpose of the tax was to fund regional assets (many of which the City of Pittsburgh funded previously), provide county tax relief, and provide support for the local municipal governments. The success of the RAD tax is viewed largely

suburbs should own up to their responsibilities and recognize that central cities are the engines of culture and economic development for most regions and that suburbanization can leave central cities with unfair social and fiscal burdens. Substantial empirical evidence shows that most central cities are drivers of a regional economy (see, for example, Sleeper, Willis, Landree, and Grill, 2004), but that has not stopped many suburbanites from fearing that regionalization, or, more specifically, consolidation, will spread the ills of the central cities to the suburbs and thus should be opposed.

---

through improved amenities (e.g., the zoo), a stable funding source for municipalities, and elimination of personal-property taxes as well as several "nuisance" taxes. However, an argument persists that imposing a tax in order to provide tax relief is an oxymoron. Critics also suggest that the RAD tax creates a fundamental inequity, forcing Allegheny County residents to pay higher taxes than do those in neighboring counties who also use the amenities and taxing residents for some services that they do not choose to use.

CHAPTER THREE

City-County Consolidation: Practitioners' and Academics' Views

Improved economic development is becoming the primary argument advanced to support city-county consolidation. So what is the evidence that consolidation will bring greater economic growth? We start with information gleaned from our interviews with economic-development practitioners and professionals around the country, then turn to the empirical academic literature. Finally, we propose our synthesis of reasons that economic development might be expected to improve with city-county consolidation.

The Practitioners

Economic-development officials and professionals we interviewed generally support city-county consolidation. We found that, in counties where consolidation had taken place, opinions about consolidation's effects on economic development ranged from mildly positive to overwhelmingly positive. In counties that had not consolidated, there was general support for the notion that consolidation would benefit economic development. Although our sample was purposive, not random, we found no commentators who said that consolidation would have a negative effect on economic development.

However, almost all the individuals we interviewed, whether in consolidated counties or not, highlighted their ability to work around obstacles of fragmented local governance, asserting, in essence, that they could still get the job done. While some of these responses undoubtedly were overly boastful and optimistic, they highlight the fact that lack of consolidation is not the only barrier that economic-development professionals face, nor is it necessarily always the most important.

Economic development takes places in a complex web of public- and private-sector interactions, and most of our commentators found it difficult to define the helpfulness of city-county consolidation to economic development. As we discuss next, the benefits are tangible (not unlike the theoretical arguments discussed previously) but difficult to measure and quantify.

The Academics

Most academics who have studied consolidation seem to believe that it will enhance planning and economic-development *capacity*—that is, the resources and skills that can be applied to improving regional economic health and well-being. Our review suggests that more rather than fewer believe it *should* help economic-development *performance*, measured, say, by job growth or other indicators of economic improvement. But remember that consolidation is a very imprecise variable, and the combination of only the City of Pittsburgh with Allegheny County government would be on the low end of the consolidation continuum. Nevertheless, the link to improved economic performance remains primarily theoretical. Insufficient empirical evidence exists to make an unequivocal statement that city-county consolidation will lead to measurable improvement in economic development.

On the other hand, there is no strong scientific analysis refuting the hypothesis that city-county consolidation can help improve regional economic development. This is a telling point, both for the proponents and opponents of consolidation. For the opponents, the small amount of empirical work that has been done tends to reinforce their predilections against consolidation. For the proponents, there is plenty of reason to believe that lack of metrics, inability to account for effects over time, and imperfect measurement are not capturing the diffuse, but real, benefits of consolidation on economic development.

We now turn to several key analyses in the academic literature that address the issues surrounding city-county consolidation and economic performance head-on.

Case Studies

In a book and an article in *Public Administration Review*, Suzanne Leland and Kurt Thurmaier (2004, 2005) presented and interpreted 12 case studies of city-county consolidation attempts, seven successful and five unsuccessful.[1] The case-study authors used a common framework as a starting point and tried to map the reality of what happened against that framework. That framework, first published in 1974 by Rosenbaum and Kammerer, sets forth a model that hypothesizes a crisis climate (including, for example, economic decline), expects so-called power deflation (loss of effectiveness of local government officials because of citizen perceptions of inadequate response to the crisis climate), and requires some kind of accelerator event (a scandal or loss of a key leader, for example) as conditions precedent to a successful consolidation election (Rosenbaum and Kammerer, 1974).

Leland and Thurmaier's (2004, 2005) work refines the Rosenbaum and Kammerer (1974) model, suggesting, among other things, that institutional context matters (e.g., the state's enabling statutes, consolidation history, number of municipalities in the county). They also distinguish between so-called development politics (the process of getting a charter commission or similar body to recommend a consolidation charter and what is required in that process) and constitutional politics (the process of convincing the voters to pass the charter and what is required in that process). They point out that the specific, detailed provisions of the proposed charter are key to eventual success at the ballot box, including issues of taxes, debt assumption, governing-body structure, treatment of smaller local governments, and responsibilities of law enforcement, among others.[2]

Their synthesis of the case studies is detailed and instructive. We touch only on a few of their points especially relevant for our discussion about economic development. First, they

---

[1]   There were 13 case studies in all, but one was really more like a city-city consolidation. The regions involved were Jacksonville (Fla.), Columbus (Ga.), Tallahassee (Fla.), Sacramento (Calif.), Athens (Ga.), Lafayette (La.), Des Moines (Iowa), Augusta-Aiken (Ga.), Wilmington (N.C.), Knoxville (Tenn.), Kansas City (Kan.), and Louisville (Ky.).

[2]   Not surprisingly, because so many of the consolidation elections have been in the southern part of the United States, support of local law enforcement (usually the elected sheriff) is imperative for successful elections.

described the importance of civic elites, not just elected officials, in the overall process—elites who take the lead in developing and selling the case for consolidation. Second, these elites include among their goals the expectation of improved economic development through better planning, the achievement of economies of scale in the development process, and improved regulatory processes for development, for example. Leland and Thurmaier (2004, 2005) observed that these arguments for the economic-development benefits of consolidation are an integral part of the case for consolidation. Third, they observed that, as opposed to economies-of-scale arguments, economic-redistribution arguments can be a death knell to voter passage of consolidation—whether or not the redistribution makes sense from an economic-development point of view. Similarly, they noted that municipalities other than the major city are virtually always left out of the consolidation—again, even when the economic-development argument for including them is compelling. Finally, for our purposes, they noted that the campaign to approve the charter must be run just as one would run a political campaign for a major office, with professional campaign staff and all the strategy, organization, creativity, and adaptability that we associate with large-scale political campaigns.

Empirical Analyses

The empirical literature exploring consolidation's effects on economic development is thin and plagued with measurement difficulties.[3] In this section, we highlight three empirical studies that have attempted to answer directly the question of whether consolidation improves economic performance. In a research note published in *State and Local Government Review*, Feiock and Carr (1997) examined the growth in business firms after the consolidation of Jacksonville and Duval County, Florida. Using modestly sophisticated analytical techniques, they concluded that consolidation did not lead to significant differences in growth in the number of firms in the retail, manufacturing, or service sectors from the growth in those sectors in the rest of the state excluding Duval County.[4] Number of firms served as a proxy for economic growth. This is not the measure one would use if other data were available, but it is at least suggestive.

Feiock and Carr (1997, p. 170) concluded,

> While economic benefits remain an important selling point for metropolitan government, our analysis failed to find evidence of a link between consolidation and economic development. No significant increases in manufacturing-, retail-, or service-sector growth were found that correspond to the consolidation of Jacksonville/Duval governments.

Two years later, in a 1999 article in *Urban Affairs*, Carr and Feiock examined the change in the number of business establishments between 1950 and 1993 in nine consolidated gov-

---

[3] First, there is no easy metric to account for the variation in what constitutes a consolidation or for the degree of consolidation and size in entities whose performance is being compared. Second, so far no one has been able to develop and use a completely satisfactory measure of economic development. Third, it has proven difficult to take account of effects over time: Consolidation is not expected to yield economic-health benefits immediately. Fourth, the crucial test is what would have happened without the intervention (in this case, consolidation). Comparing performance after consolidation between a consolidated entity and the rest of the state is an imperfect measure. Also, the business cycle and general economic conditions fluctuate, as does the mix of industries and businesses in a region; picking start and end times given economic fluctuations and comparing structurally different local economies can affect the outcomes.

[4] Consolidation became effective in 1968. Data were available from 1950 to 1993. The preconsolidation period was 1950–1968, and 1973–1993 was considered the postconsolidation period, allowing for a five-year period for consolidation effects, if any, to become fully realized. See Feiock and Carr (1997).

ernments. The consolidations took place between 1967 and 1984, so data were available for before and after consolidation. They used essentially the same analytical techniques as they had for the earlier article. Firms were classed as manufacturing or retail/services, giving 18 time series of data to be analyzed. Seven of the 18 series showed statistically significant increased growth postconsolidation, although a majority did not (11 of the 18). This can be interpreted as mildly positive support for the notion that consolidation can enhance economic development. However, the next stage of the analysis asked whether any of the seven cases showing positive growth postconsolidation had growth significantly different from that of the state in which they were located. In the words of Carr and Feiock (1999, p. 481), "[N]one of the consolidated counties experienced a change in economic development that was statistically different from the statewide trend over the same period." They also said, however, that "the creation of the consolidated government did not *reduce* [their emphasis] economic growth in the county in any of these cases."

Finally, in 2006, Carr, Bae, and Lu compared the postconsolidation growth patterns of Lexington–Fayette County, Kentucky, to then-unconsolidated Louisville and Jefferson County, Kentucky. Expectation of improved economic development was a vital part of the argument for consolidating Knoxville and Jefferson County during the 2000 charter vote,[5] so the question naturally arises whether the consolidation of Lexington and Fayette County in 1972 had indeed improved their economic development relative to the then-unconsolidated Knoxville and Jefferson County.

The short answer: Mostly no.

Extending the methodology of the earlier work somewhat, Carr, Bae, and Lu (2006) measured growth in the number of firms in three sectors: manufacturing, retail, and service, each divided into six groupings by employee size. They also measured total payroll growth for the three sectors. The data cover 1950–1997. The division of firms into six groups by size and the measurement of total payroll in the three sectors in part answered criticism of the earlier Carr and Feiock (1999) analysis that implicitly treated all firms as if they had the same impact on growth.

The analysis created 42 so-called models (21 for each site), reflecting the six firm-size groupings by three sector groupings, as well as total payroll data for each of the three sectors. Five of these models showed statistically significant improvement in growth in Lexington-Fayette after consolidation, but only three of the models showed improvement greater than that seen in then-unconsolidated Knoxville-Jefferson. As Carr, Bae, and Lu (2006, p. 265) summarized,

> [T]hese findings show that the development benefits that can be attributed to the city-county government in Lexington-Fayette are limited to retail establishments with fewer than 50 employees and service establishments with 100–249 employees. The findings of this study provide little support for the contention that the adoption of city-county government substantially altered the development patterns in Lexington-Fayette that existed prior to the merger of its city and county governments. Indeed, they confirm earlier analyses showing no systematic development improvements from city-county government.

---

[5] In fact, Carr, Bae, and Lu (2006) began their article with a quote from Savitch and Vogel (1999, p. 4): "Louisville's haunting fear is that Lexington-Fayette will overtake it during the early part of the next century." We heard that fear repeated as a motivating factor in the charter election when we visited Louisville in July 2007.

But even this somewhat improved analysis still faced the difficulties mentioned previously. Carr, Bae, and Lu (2006, p. 267) pointed out that "[e]mpirical studies that focus on different sets of communities and employ different research approaches are needed to better understand the implications of substantial reorganization of local governments."

Carr and Feiock (1999) offered possible explanations for their conclusion that no link was observed between consolidation and economic improvement—at least none that may be useful to think about in the Pittsburgh context. Accepting as plausible that consolidation does improve the professionalism, planning capacity, and the legal, jurisdictional, and financial resources available to local government, they asked why that is not translated into greater economic growth. They posited two broad explanations: first, that consolidation may reduce some of the inefficiencies of the economic-development process stemming from competition among local governments and booster organizations in a region. That is, the region may not bid up incentives for attracting new jobs and may not provide duplicative services but may instead experience the same amount of development that would have occurred anyway but at lower public cost. Second, the charters put to the voters may involve so many compromises to help passage that there is insufficient consolidation and integration of functions necessary to overcome a fragmented approach to regional economic development. Leaving many municipalities and special governments out of a consolidation attempt may thwart the realization of metropolitan planning and coordination of economic-development efforts.

Other scholars might suggest that entirely different variables could account for these studies' inability to identify convincing effects. For example, in a study of a large economic-development program in Minnesota, Margaret Dewar (1998) determined that the program's success or failure was attributable in large measure to what she termed *bureaucratic and political imperatives*. That is, politicians responding to their constituencies and the need for quick results and bureaucrats sensitive to the needs of their bosses and norms of bureaucratic behavior (not the least of which is survival) will shape and form economic-development activities and programs in ways that likely have little to do with technical efficiency.

We end here by returning to a provocative observation from the studies: Consolidated regions that showed statistically significant improvement in economic-development rates performed at least as well as the average trends for the state where they were located. While researchers viewed this as the absence of success, it also suggests that these regions would have lagged behind the progress in their respective states without these significant improvements.

The Economic-Development Case

This chapter turns to the main focus of our discussion of consolidation: whether it fosters economic development. It begins by laying out what are seen as the goals of economic development and turns next to ways of measuring economic improvement.

The Goals of Economic Development

The generally acknowledged goal of economic development is a healthy economy. Traditionally, that has meant that economic-development departments and boosters were tasked with attracting new jobs to a region, primarily from firms and institutions outside of the region. However, a number of elements of a region contribute to a healthy economy, and each element can be a focus of improvement efforts that contribute to successful economic development.

Among the most important elements are general *quality-of-life* conditions, such as climate, quality of schools, crime, recreational opportunities, tax burdens, infrastructure (such as transportation, sewage treatment, and water supply), housing availability and pricing, and cultural and recreational opportunities. All of these elements contribute to a community's attractiveness, and many are measured in the frequently published ratings of best cities or regions in the country. (See, for example, Sperling and Sander, 2007; Savageau, 2007.)

Another set of important elements includes the region's actual and potential workforces. Most economic-development organizations track demographics and skill mix of workers, and growth in people or jobs generally has been seen as a positive indicator of economic development. Often, special attention is paid to the needs of one sector or another (high-tech jobs, for example) or to specific demographic groups (need more, younger workers in a region).

A third key aspect of a healthy economy is the type and range of existing businesses and institutions and the nature of commerce in a region. Increasingly, those responsible for economic development point to the importance of nurturing firms and institutions already in the region and helping firms increase their capacity to grow and innovate within the region. This is sometimes referred to as being a business-friendly or hassle-free community.

It is useful to note these different bundles of economic activity and the environment in which they operate because, as we look to the potential effects of city-county consolidation on economic development, we want to remember that there are many aspects of the everyday care and feeding of the economy that may not fall into traditional concepts of economic development but that consolidation might nevertheless affect—thus indirectly helping or hurting the regional economy's health.

Identifying the elements of a healthy economy leads naturally to a set of goals for economic development. We group these into three bundles: Nurture the existing economy; attract new business firms and institutions to the region; and maintain and enhance the attractiveness of the workforce.

Nurture the Existing Economy

Improve schools, reduce crime, reduce tax burdens, improve cultural and recreational opportunities, reduce congestion, increase the diversity and affordability of housing choices, and *maintain a safe and plentiful water supply* are examples of goals that may be spread among various governments and institutions in the region. Rarely would these be the goals of an economic-development department, per se, but progress on such goals as these reinforces and amplifies the specific goals of the economic-development professionals. To the extent that consolidation of a city and county would be expected to lead to measurable improvement in goals such as these, one would expect an indirectly positive effect on the regional economy.

Similarly, goals that focus on making it easy for existing businesses and institutions to develop and grow (such as improving information sharing among small businesses and government, streamlining the process for acquiring various permits, reducing barriers to expansion, and simplifying rules and regulations for business operations) support the larger goal of regional economic development—whether or not an economic-development department or authority is involved. The goal is to make the process for business establishment and growth as transparent as possible.

Another essential part of the goal structure for economic development is to help existing businesses or start-up businesses innovate and blossom. Providing incubator facilities and investment funds through such organizations as the Pittsburgh Life Sciences Greenhouse are examples of this. As one observer put it during our interviews, 10 years from now, many—perhaps even a majority—of the employees in the region will work for firms that do not exist today.

Attract New Firms and Institutions (Jobs) to the Region

This, of course, is what most people think about when they think about the mission of economic development. The focus is outside the region and typically, but certainly not exclusively, on larger firms seen as drivers of an economy. Traditionally, but perhaps less so now, this is where site-selection consultants and other intermediaries play large roles. The number of firms looking to move very large numbers of jobs, however, is quite small. Although such firms can be extremely important to an economy, the likelihood of bringing a very large employer to a region is therefore very small also. Nevertheless, since the most common metric for success in economic development is job growth, the search for large employers outside the region long has been a mainstay of economic-development efforts.

That focus has evolved as manufacturing jobs have declined and service jobs have increased. Smaller and mid-sized firms are being sought, especially those with strong growth potential, as well as firms in specific sectors that complement existing firms or build on comparative advantages of a region. A particularly popular thrust has been the search for high-tech or knowledge-industry jobs, following the example of Silicon Valley and some other regions of the country. But regions strong in other sectors seek to build on their strengths also, a good example being the health-care sector in Pittsburgh.

Clustering of interdependent firms may lower costs of production, and clustering of competing firms may increase the number of suppliers (potentially lowering the cost of production) and bring more customers who appreciate the diversity and selection of a particular product or service. This economic concept of agglomeration economies seems to withstand the test of time as more examples are studied and validated.[1]

Part of the arsenal of economic development has been the provision of various incentive packages, such as tax abatement, publicly funded infrastructure improvements, and other subventions. Grants scaled to the number of jobs created are not uncommon, and now some regions even monitor the pace of job creation and pay only on verification that the number of jobs promised is actually created.

Maintain and Enhance the Local Workforce

Economic-development professionals have always known that the nature and quality of the local labor force is key to developing and maintaining a growing local economy. However, it has only been in the past two decades or so that the focus of economic-development professionals has broadened away from seeking *firms* that had jobs with desirable workforces to attempting also to attract or create *employees* with desirable job traits. This search for talent and human capital highlights the importance of various place-based characteristics of the local economy (Currid, 2007).

The economic folklore is that, if you create the jobs, people will come. Nevertheless, economic-development professionals have found that, if they do not pay attention to what keeps the workforce in a region, they may lose that workforce. And, similarly, if the existing workforce lacks the skills that are attractive to firms, some kind of retraining or upgrading of skills is needed. This is a classic chicken-and-egg problem: "If we don't have the jobs, we won't attract the workers. If our existing workers aren't attractive to employers, we won't attract the jobs."

The Pittsburgh region knows these lessons all too well, having faced one of the more dramatic declines in manufacturing jobs in the country while also generating one of the most impressive potential new workforces in the graduates of its many colleges and universities. However, keeping a greater proportion of graduates in the region, attracting graduates from colleges and universities outside the region, and attracting younger workers to the region remains a formidable challenge—a challenge that presumably would be high on the list of goals for a consolidated city-county government.

The goals for economic development can be stated in many complex ways, but the metrics typically used to gauge success against these goals are relatively few. Tellingly, in the words of one our interviewees, "No matter what they say about other goals, it always comes back to jobs, jobs, jobs." We now turn to a discussion of measuring economic improvement.

Measuring Economic Improvement

The strength of the economy and the success of economic development usually have been measured by only a few metrics—firm growth by sector, job growth, and net or gross product. As

---

[1] See, for example, Currid (2007) for a recent study on how agglomeration economies are important to art and culture in New York City.

noted previously, however, success of a regional economy may be measured across many outcomes that are related to a broad set of factors. Though challenging to identify and measure, it is useful to track indicators both for regional outcomes and for contributing factors. Once identified, these indicators establish *a regional baseline*, measuring the progress of regional development, and even comparing a region to a set of benchmark communities. A number of organizations in Pittsburgh track various metrics for measuring the economy, and it is not the purpose of this report to replicate or extend that work.[2] Rather, we briefly review measures here in the context of thinking about how city-county consolidation might be assessed.

Table 4.1 presents some indicators of economic performance. Direct measures of economic performance move with the economy (e.g., an increase in the number of jobs over a period is taken as a direct reflection of a stronger local economy). Similarly, rising per-capita income generally is thought of as desirable evidence of an improving economy—and one that can support better government services. Alternatively, lower tax rates often are seen as a positive measure.

The absolute changes in indicators are important for a region to know, but the relative changes are equally critical. Per-capita income may rise steadily, but does it surpass the rate of inflation, increasing more quickly or slowly than surrounding communities, similar regions, the state, or country? And even more subtly, is per-capita income rising simply because population is declining, as appears to be the case in the Pittsburgh area?[3]

Indirect measures of economic performance are those that are correlated with regional economic success or failure. Demographic, cultural, and environmental conditions can affect the perceived quality of a region, which, in turn, may affect economic-development opportunities.

Unfortunately, few studies test the relationships between the factors in Table 4.1 and the form of governance. We found evidence in the literature of a relationship between governance structure and three *direct* performance metrics. Sometimes the evidence supported a

Table 4.1
Economic-Performance Indicators

Direct	Indirect
Employment and job growth rate	Labor-force characteristics and skill mix
Unemployment rate	Housing availability and price
Per-capita income	School quality and educational opportunity
Quantity of building permits issued	Infrastructure quality and efficiency
Median salary growth	Environmental quality
Migration rates	Business-friendly environment
Gross regional product	Venture-capital investment
Tax and service-fee burdens	Entertainment and cultural resources
Industrial mix	Demographic distribution

---

[2]   For examples, see PittsburghToday (undated) and Pittsburgh's Future (undated).

[3]   See, for example, Miller (2007).

positive relationship with consolidated governance, other times with fragmented governance, and occasionally with both types of structures. We briefly describe the empirical support for some of these factors next.

- *Employment and job growth rate*: Feiock and Carr (1997) found a positive but statistically insignificant relationship between the number of jobs pre- and postconsolidation.
- *Per-capita income*: There is positive but not statistically significant evidence of a relationship between government consolidation and income growth (Nelson and Foster, 1999). Feiock and Carr (1997) suggested that their analyses strongly support increases in per-capita income as a result of consolidation. Foster (1993) found inconclusive results linking the two.
- *Taxes and Service Fees*: Researchers report some evidence in support of consolidated governance and reduced taxes and service fees. The theoretical arguments go both ways. On one hand, total costs may be reduced in consolidated governments through increased efficiencies, translating into lower taxes and fees.[4] However, other researchers suggest that people and businesses are better able to select their most effective mix of taxes and fees when there are more governments in an area, since each can choose where to locate within a region based on their preferred level of services and the associated costs (Adams, 1965; Isserman, 1976; Sjoquist, 1982; Nelson, 1987; Schneider, 1989). This argument is frequently cited (though not exclusively) locally as the reason for flight from the city to the suburbs and to adjacent counties.

The limited empirical evidence is mixed. Eberts and Gronber (1988), for example, examined the county and metropolitan-area relationship and their local-government expenditures in local markets. They found negligible change or increase in costs caused by higher numbers of single-purpose (consolidated) governments in an area. In general, the evidence mostly is that consolidation is not likely to reduce taxes and fees.

Thus, as discussed earlier, the case for or against city-county consolidation has to be made on grounds other than scientific empirical research.

Elements of the Economic-Development Case

Through readings and interviews, we have identified several characteristics that are cited frequently as support for the proposition that city-county consolidation can improve regional economic development. These salient elements of the economic-development case are listed in Table 4.2. We have referred to them earlier in our review of the literature, and most were mentioned in each of our interviews. Although we cannot readily measure differences in these elements with and without consolidation, certainly it is the perception of practitioners, theorists, and involved citizens with whom we have talked that these results of consolidation can and do make a difference in economic performance.

---

[4] See, e.g., see Stephens and Wikstrom (2000), Nelson (1986), and Eberts and Gronberg (1988).

Table 4.2
Salient Elements of an Economic-Development Case

Category	Element
Unity of leadership	One accountable decisionmaker Common vision; speak with one voice Greater regional stature Improved access to state and federal money
Increased planning and development capacity	More-comprehensive planning and coordinated land-use regulation Improved public-private cooperation Larger legal and resource base for attracting and supporting development More-sophisticated economic-development capability
Simpler regulatory procedures for business	Clarity of authority Improved transparency Streamlined permit processing
Reduced intergovernmental competition	Less-fragmented governance Fewer inefficient economic-development subsidies

Unity of Leadership

This is a broad category that centers on the notions of clarity and rationality. Virtually all our respondents stressed the importance to economic development of having a common vision and one clearly accountable decisionmaker. It is disconcerting to businesses and citizens when local political leaders with different agendas appear to be impeding progress—granted, the definition of *progress* is in the eye of the beholder. Few businesses want to invest in a tumultuous political environment in which uncertainty is high. County and city governments have different constituencies, and, although they may cooperate in many ways, they usually have fundamental differences in purpose, scale, and style that sooner or later put them at odds with each other in ways that are apparent to firms wanting to invest in the region.

Our respondents talked about this generally and in terms of large public-infrastructure projects especially. "We never could have built the stadium." "The racetrack never would have located here." "This redevelopment would not have happened." These phrases were accompanied with the tag "unless we were consolidated," or more directly, "as long as the city and county leaders chose to go their separate ways."

Some consolidated areas also tout enhanced regional stature, usually by population size, from the simple fact of consolidation. "We went from being the 59th to 11th largest metropolitan area in the United States," or some similar improvement goes the refrain. We did not find a lot of support for this argument, but regions do keep score against each other, and self-image is important to economic development. *Bigger is better*, or at least *bigger than we are at the moment is better*, is a common thread of economic development. Consolidation undeniably provides bragging rights about size, but the size of the region was there before consolidation, and, most likely, the relabeling of that size is not what brings increased economic development, if it comes.

Enhanced access to state and federal dollars also is part of the case for consolidation. However, our interviews provided contrasting arguments for this. The predominant argument on the one hand is that funding may increase if a unified, coordinated case for economic development is presented to funding entities for a region. However, we found a minority but strongly voiced view that state or federal funding agencies may expect that a unified region will achieve efficiencies, thus enabling the entity to do more with less funding than two (or more) entities would need separately. A corollary to this is the view we also heard, that governments have many cooperative efforts already and that a new entity may look little different to state and federal funders, thereby suggesting little change in state and local funding.

Increased Planning and Development Capability

Whereas practitioners and locals who have been through consolidation tend to mention unity of leadership frequently, the theorists and promoters of metropolitan government often cite increased planning and development capability as a strong argument for consolidation. As part of their examination of the consolidation of the City of Jacksonville and Duval County, Florida, discussed earlier, Carr and Feiock (1999) found that dealing with one consolidated government improved the available planning capacity and the legal, jurisdictional, and financial resources available. With these additional resources, the consolidated government's planning was enhanced, and coordinated development across the area became more feasible.

In a broader look at governance and economic performance, Hamilton, Miller, and Paytas (2004) found that governance affects the long-term competitiveness of a local economy. They argued that governance does not determine economic outcomes directly but reduces a region's ability to *adapt*. This is another version of the capacity or capability argument.

Indianapolis is cited as an example in which consolidation encouraged the formation of public-private partnerships for economic development and increased success in obtaining development grants (Rusk, 1993, as cited in Feiock and Carr, 1997). In short, the argument says that increased resources and a common vision yield a more sophisticated economic-development strategy—such as enhanced public-private partnerships—and thus lead to greater economic growth. Although the empirical studies and techniques for validating that logic chain have not kept pace with the perceptions that it is correct, we found general support for that chain of logic in our interviews.

Simpler Regulatory Procedures for Business

Economic-development professionals place high value on the extent to which a region is a business-friendly community. How difficult is it for a business to obtain information about permits, zoning, taxes, incentives, and so forth in a locale? When an issue arises, how many decisionmakers control or contribute to its outcome? There is some evidence that fragmented governance can have negative consequences for new development when the fragmentation adds to confusion, delays, and uncertainty due to the need to gain approvals from multiple departments (Feiock, 1994). With multiple governments, the number of approvals and permits is increased, extending the approval process for some types of development (Feiock and Carr, 1997). Wolfson and Frisken (2000) found empirical support for regional approaches to local governance allowing for more-effective decisionmaking processes. (See also Lembeck, Kelsey, and Fasic, 2001.)

The studies in this area suggest that consolidated or regional approaches to governing the economic-development function *may* create environments that are friendlier to businesses. However, as we noted earlier, our respondents both inside and outside the Pittsburgh region suggested that economic-development professionals working with many governmental units find workarounds to get things done, sometimes creating an illusion of unity and transparency. These workarounds, however, can mask inefficiency and do not solve the need for transparency.

One community, for example, assigns one individual to work with a firm all the way through the process of expressing interest in expanding or bringing jobs into the region, helping the firm get whatever new license, zoning change, building permit, tax incentive, or whatever is required to begin operations. This approach is contrasted to another approach to streamlining the permit process: one-stop shopping. Here, the goal is for applicants, especially for property-related information and permits, to go to only one location, where all the applicable permits can be processed. Whatever approach is used to streamline the process, economic-development staff tend to adapt and to eliminate the barriers to speedy, effective processing where they can. Nevertheless, despite the creativity of various workarounds, a reasonable case can be made that consolidation can improve economic-development regulatory procedures.

Reduced Intergovernmental Competition

There are at least two parts to this element of the case: (1) less-fragmented government will lead to improved economic development, and (2) the region will not provide inefficient subsidies resulting from local competition for new development.

Starting with the second part, multiple jurisdictions within a local area result in a market of governments that allows companies interested in the area to pit local government units against one another (Lind, 1997). Although this may ultimately result in better tax exemptions or other incentives for a specific firm, the larger regional effects may be negative rather than positive. For example, a firm may take advantage of a local-government offer to provide tax abatement as well as to provide a new road that parallels an underused road in an adjacent municipality. That firm may benefit, but creating overcapacity in a portion of a regional transportation system with serious undercapacity in other areas where those resources could have been used leads to a less desirable result for the region as a whole—and, following the logic— unnecessary gridlock that may ultimately reduce the region's attractiveness to growth.

The degree of intergovernmental competition can affect the level of taxes in a region, as already noted, in addition to affecting economic development. A jurisdiction relying on business-income taxes within its boundaries to provide services, for example, has incentives to compete with neighbors near and far to sustain or increase its own revenues. Such competition can have a deleterious effect on economic development when businesses pit jurisdictions against each other to obtain tax breaks that may negate benefits to local taxpayers or absorb scarce local-government resources of time and money used to vie for development projects. The conclusion that resources used for economic development will be better deployed under jurisdictions in which there is less local-government fragmentation and accompanying local-government competition has strong appeal.

CHAPTER FIVE

Consolidating the City of Pittsburgh and Allegheny County

We now turn to assessing how the elements of the economic-development case fare in the Pittsburgh–Allegheny County setting. Conceptually, we want to retrace the arguments and assess where the balance might fall specifically for Pittsburgh–Allegheny County. We begin with a simple recounting of the elements of the economic-development case set forth in Table 4.2 in Chapter Four. Table 5.1 shows the elements based on our assessment of the body of evidence of differences that might show up when comparing an unconsolidated City of Pittsburgh and Allegheny County to a consolidated entity These assessments are based on the theoretical and empirical literature, case studies, and interviews with practitioners. Our intent is to signal the direction of change, if any, and the intensity that might be expected. Since there is so

Table 5.1
Elements of an Economic-Development Case and Anticipated Effect from Consolidation of the City of Pittsburgh and Allegheny County

Element	Characteristic	Anticipated Effect of Consolidation on Characteristic
Unity of leadership	One accountable decisionmaker	Greatly improve
	Common vision; speak with one voice	Greatly improve
	Greater regional stature	No change
	Improved access to state and federal money	Likely no change
Increased planning and development capacity	More-comprehensive planning and coordinated land-use regulation	Improve
	Improved public-private cooperation	No change
	Larger legal and resource base for attracting and supporting development	Improve
	More-sophisticated economic-development capability	Little or no change
Simpler regulatory procedures for business	Clarity of authority	Improve
	Improved transparency	Improve
	Streamlined permit processing	Little or no change
Reduced intergovernmental competition	Less-fragmented governance	Improve
	Fewer inefficient economic-development subsidies	No change

little empirical evidence to guide us, these assessments obviously are our informed judgments based on the information we collected and reviewed. We discuss the elements in turn.

Unity of Leadership

Having one accountable decisionmaker is among the strongest arguments that consolidation will improve economic development over time. Both theorists and practitioners cite enough examples of success to make this a reasonable hypothesis. Case studies and interviews provide evidence of stagnating development that resulted when a mayor and county executive were out of step or actively engaged in competition. In these cases, consolidation provided a single leader who was able to broker development that had not been possible in the past. At present, two officials who work well together lead the City of Pittsburgh and Allegheny County. However, this has not always been the case, nor is there any reason to believe that a mayor and executive will be politically or philosophically united on economic-development issues. The case is marginalized somewhat by the fact that a consolidation of the City of Pittsburgh and Allegheny County government is only one step in the direction of having one accountable decisionmaker. With the large number of municipalities not included in such a consolidation, the county—let alone the region—still will have more than 100 municipal leaders, each with a constituency to be served. Nevertheless, this argument is compelling based on the information we collected and reviewed.

The notions of a common vision and speaking (comparatively) with one voice and the notion of one accountable decisionmaker are parts of the same fundamental argument. The argument is appealing intuitively and again was validated through case studies and practitioner interviews. It has advocates in regions where consolidation has taken place, generates regrets about fragmented decisionmaking from observers in regions where consolidation has not taken place but is seen as desirable, and has promoters of regionalism in general behind it. The argument falls into the broader class of a search for clarity and rationality. However, lingering beneath all these arguments is the question of whether progress would have been made anyway with or without consolidation or may just have taken longer to achieve the same outcome. As already discussed, we lack the empirical evidence to be definitive on the topic, but the weight of evidence suggests that consolidation can have a large effect on creating a more unifying voice for a region.

Our judgment is that these first two characteristics under unity of leadership would make a strongly positive difference in the Pittsburgh–Allegheny County case. The Pittsburgh region—despite frequently voiced self-doubts—is a major urban region in the United States with many assets and strong public-private partnerships. But fragmentation does complicate economic development across the county, and the city and county per force must serve different constituencies, inevitably leading to political differences about economic-development strategies as a structural matter. Thus, although these two elements are by no means the whole case for or against consolidation of the city and the county, they suggest a noticeably positive outcome for economic development under consolidation.

As discussed in Chapter Three, the regional-stature issue is mostly a feel-good issue that can help local boosters and can make the region's population feel more positive about the region. The most common thread of this argument is that consolidation will improve a region's ranking in population listings and thus attract more attention to prospective economic development in the region. Our respondents and economic-development professionals, however, did not feel that using the county population figure (resulting from the consolidation) would materially affect economic development. Seasoned economic-development professionals know how to decipher population data, and the region already has population figures that are much larger than the simple combination of the city and county statistics. The population of the Pittsburgh MSA, for example, is about 2.3 million, already substantially greater than Allegheny County's 1.2 million. And in this age of the Internet, anyone can access the fact quickly that the population in both those areas has been declining. There is no compelling case in the literature or from experts that a greater regional stature stemming from consolidation will have any measurable impact on future economic development. Thus, our judgment is that, on this characteristic, one could expect the same economic-development future with or without consolidation. But we note that the region starts from a strong base already. Despite population and job declines, Pittsburgh has many attractions for economic development, and those attractions can be exploited with or without consolidation.

Improved access to state and local funding is—as they say—too close to call. The evidence for this judgment is from economic-development experts in the region and state. Some Pittsburgh observers suggest that a combined Pittsburgh and Allegheny County would gain better access to the statehouse in Harrisburg. Other observers expressed skepticism that this would be the case. All the individuals we interviewed who take part in seeking money from the state and federal governments said that they felt that the cooperation in approaching outside funding sources was reasonably good in the Pittsburgh region. They doubted that consolidation would lead to increased funding—despite suggestions that this might be or has been the case elsewhere. Finally, as noted in Chapter Three, some experts suggested that federal and state funding could go down if funding sources perceive that the larger entity is better able to take care of itself. We did not pursue this issue with legislators or federal or state funding sources. However, based on what we heard from those with whom we did talk, our judgment is that consolidation likely would lead to little change in either access or likely amount of economic-development funding directly or funding that indirectly would help economic development. Thus, we show likely no change in Table 5.1 on the characteristic of improved access to state and federal funds under the element or category of unity of leadership. Our judgment could change if more municipalities were included in a consolidation, because—almost by definition—many of the smaller municipalities could gain increased access through the larger government.

Increased Planning and Development Capacity

On balance, we would expect to see modest improvement in economic development when measured by change in the characteristics grouped under the category of increased planning and development capacity. As noted already, the Pittsburgh region has significant examples of public-private cooperation, and we do not see consolidation of the city and county as changing that noticeably, nor did we hear talk of that in our interviews with local practitioners. However, most of our respondents (and we) do see opportunities for some modest improvement in terms of more-comprehensive planning and coordinated land-use regulation, somewhat more sophisticated economic-development capability, and the potential power of a combined resource base for attracting development.

The SPC undertakes substantial regional-planning efforts in fulfillment of its responsibilities as a federally mandated metropolitan planning organization, and, as of this writing, Allegheny County is launching a major update of its general plan. The City of Pittsburgh historically has had a robust city-planning capacity that is now somewhat diminished, given fiscal constraints. Based on the literature on regional development and some empirical studies,[1] combining the city and county does provide an opportunity to strengthen comprehensive planning for the city and county and to improve coordination of land-use regulations. Even recognizing that most of the authorities that affect economic development, such as the city's Urban Redevelopment Authority, would not change, combining the city's and county's planning and economic-development efforts sets a stage for increased coherence in planning efforts and thus, indirectly, increased coherence in economic development. Our assessment in Table 5.1 suggests modest improvement, which also reflects what we heard from local experts in our interviews. There would be a larger difference if more of the other county municipalities were involved, especially since there is a strong perception that conflicting or inadequate land-use regulations across the municipalities hinder economic development.

We also see modest opportunity for improvement that can come from a larger legal and resource base for attracting development. Based on the literature and interviews with practitioners, this argument mostly flows from the potential reduction in competition and potential increase in coordination between city and county, as well as the increased presence that a combined city and county could make compared with other counties in the region and other regions in the country. However, Pittsburgh and Allegheny County already have significant economic-development presence, albeit fragmented somewhat, across several institutions. Consolidation should help sharpen and clarify economic-development goals and programs and, in doing so, potentially create opportunities for more funding to support economic development, but we suspect that any increase would be modest.

Finally, we also see opportunity, as do some of our respondents, for increased sophistication in economic-development capability from consolidation. This argument enters the literature in circumstances in which there are large differences in capability between the entities being consolidated and the underresourced areas gain an immediate boost with consolidation. That is not the case in Pittsburgh. But the complex and evolving array of counties, cities, authorities, and regional planning organizations, let alone the state and federal governments, involved in economic development in southwestern Pennsylvania can be overwhelming to someone either trying to understand options for bringing economic development to the region or trying to fashion sensible programs to attract development. Combining the city and the county is a small step that can help rationalize economic-development efforts of the two separate entities and their interactions with the many players in economic development, as well as yield, potentially, more-powerful and -coherent strategies. The area of workforce development, to pick only one example, might be a case in which a combined city and county speaking as one voice with reach across the entire county could fashion more-sophisticated approaches than each entity would do alone—even though almost any economic-development program undertaken by the separate entities can be characterized as involving cooperation or coordination with the other entity as appropriate now. Thus, we do not want to overstate the case; but we do see a possible positive effect from consolidation on this characteristic of the case.

---

[1]   See, for example, Brookings Institution (2003).

Simpler Regulatory Procedures for Business

The most common comments we heard about regulatory procedures as impediments to economic development in the Pittsburgh region centered on navigating procedures across two or more municipalities—for example, when undertaking a development that would cross boundaries or installing an infrastructure project that crosses boundaries. Consolidation of the city and county could ease those impediments, perhaps with a redesigned property-development permit-processing procedure. But the literature and interviews did not yield salient examples in which the permitting process for property-related matters as between the city and the county alone was a serious impediment. What we heard tended to be focused on issues outside the City of Pittsburgh (although, in some eyes, the recent casino-development process revealed opportunities for improvement). We would not expect much change toward a streamlined property-development permit processing with a city-county consolidation without a whole new program designed by the new entity with streamlining specifically in mind.

There seems to be a common perception among local experts that economic-development assistance writ large in the southwestern Pennsylvania area (e.g., getting business licenses easily, accessing tax-abatement programs, receiving subsidies for infrastructure improvements, gaining entry to workforce-improvement programs) is difficult to understand and the processes difficult to navigate. That is a problem on which the region needs to work with or without city-county consolidation. But for the mainline property-development functions, a consolidated entity would need to introduce far more-sweeping reforms than just a combination of offices to make a dent in the perceived problem. And even then, with so many other permitting agencies not involved in the consolidation, we judge, in concert with most of our respondents, that city-county consolidation likely would produce little change on this metric.

However, for the two other characteristics in this category, clarity of authority and improved transparency, consolidation provides an opportunity for modest gains based on our assessment of the literature. The clarity-of-authority argument is similar to the unity-of-leadership one except that it is focused on outsiders to a region. In particular, clarity of authority makes it easy for businesses and others, who do not know the region's politics, to identify a focal point for entry into the system and to track relevant policies and practices. Although the specific policies of the City of Pittsburgh are not always germane to someone trying to locate or grow a business in a suburban municipality still within Allegheny County, consolidation can reduce an important layer of confusion about points of entry into the system and smooth the distinctions between development in or outside of the current boundaries of the City of Pittsburgh. We say this acknowledging that other municipalities within the county and other towns and counties within the region taken together still make the Pittsburgh region one of the most fragmented metropolitan regions in the country when measured by number of governance units.

Under consolidation, the theoretical literature points to some possibility for improved transparency in processes relative to economic development. In the age of agency Web pages and electronic government services, citizens and participants in the community are provided with tremendous amounts of information, but few have the time or inclination to compare regulations and programs across jurisdictions or to create a road map on their own of all the regulations or programs that might be relevant to their proposed actions. Those who do search both the city and county Web sites for relevant information can struggle with similar-sounding names for different activities or an unrecognized name for an activity that would be relevant to their needs. For the most part, the city and the county are not going to provide pointers to all the other relevant jurisdictions or programs that may be relevant.

Accordingly, the opaqueness of processes is one reason that there are economic-development professionals in the city and county and in the various nongovernmental-organization economic-development support groups. Still, firms and institutions must be able to do large parts of the job on their own. Reducing two entities with large regulatory roles to one entity and then making sure that the regulatory schemes are not just layered on top of each other with no change has the potential to increase the transparency of government and, in the long run, improve economic development. Even mindful of implementation issues that arise in combining regulatory schemes, as well as the danger that a larger entity can add bureaucratic roadblocks, we think that consolidation of the City of Pittsburgh and Allegheny County could yield improvement on the metrics of clarity of authority and improved transparency.

Reduced Intergovernmental Competition

The theoretical literature on governance notes a hypothesized negative impact of intergovernmental competition (from fragmented governance) on economic development. Local interviews throughout the region spoke to the topic as well, but we heard relatively little—which is not to say nothing—about the competition directly between the city and the county. Representatives of the city and county point out that they have different constituencies to serve but, in the end, want the region to grow. Therefore, a job outside the city but within the county or a job outside the county but within the region is better than no job in the region at all, so the saying goes. But as already noted, the Pittsburgh region is a large place with lots going on. Simply fulfilling duties to their constituencies creates competition between the city and the county. That is especially true for the county, since it must support all the municipalities in its boundaries. It cannot be Pittsburgh-centric and survive in the long run.

It is extremely hard to measure the degree that economic-development competition between the city and county may be destructive rather than healthy. Our judgment is that consolidation will reduce somewhat the competition between the two entities but that, when viewed from the perspective of the region as a whole, there likely will be no or very little discernable change in intergovernmental competition.

The metric of reducing inefficient development subsidies comes primarily from the theoretical literature. The practical reality comes from multiple municipalities bidding up the savings to firms entering the region or seeking to enlarge within the region but not necessarily within the same jurisdiction. A recent case perceived to be on point—we did not verify the details of the cases made—in the Pittsburgh region is the expansion of part of the Westinghouse Corporation. A planned expansion ended up in a neighboring county within the region, not Allegheny County. The extent to which Allegheny County should have or even could have provided enticements to keep the expansion within the county was the subject of considerable public speculation during Westinghouse's decisionmaking process. The point for our purposes is not whether the outcome was correct but that the reality is that jurisdictions will compete for jobs and tax base, and theory suggests that, in the end, competition will bid up the cost of subsidies to local government.

We conclude that this characteristic would show no discernable change with or without consolidation because, as far as we could determine, consolidation of only the city and county would not materially change the nature of the competition among jurisdictions in the region in such a way that economic development would clearly be enhanced. Consolidation among the county, Pittsburgh, and more of the other jurisdictions in the county likely would have some measurable effects. But the Westinghouse expansion is a cautionary tale in that regard. Competition among the counties in the region would continue even if all the jurisdictions within Allegheny County were consolidated with the county. The recognition that southwestern Pennsylvania competes with other regions in the United States and should be perceived, planned, and promoted as a region is voiced, but that does not stop localities within the region from seeking what they think is best for themselves. This reality attenuates one's ability to suggest the degree to which reduced intergovernmental competition within parts of a region will bring enhanced economic development to that part of the region.

Putting the Case Together

Our analysis suggests that some characteristics of each element of the economic-development case for consolidation could make a contribution to improved economic development of the Pittsburgh region. One accountable decisionmaker providing the leadership and discipline to generate a common vision and the opportunity for the region to speak with one voice regarding economic development has potential to enhance the region's economic development. Many observers, academics and practitioners alike, believe that consolidation can bring increased capacity to deliver improved land-use planning and economic-development services to a region, and that appears to be possible in the Pittsburgh region. Finally, consolidation holds a promise of improving the transparency of governmental economic-development operations and potentially reducing some of the ills of fragmented governance.

The direction and strength of elements of a possible case for improved economic development through consolidation that we have identified are noncommensurable. We are not proposing that one simply sum the elements that are hypothesized to improve with consolidation and declare the case to have been made. The elements overlap somewhat and could not survive a rigorous factor analysis as truly independent factors. They are distillations of arguments found in the literature, case studies, and interviews with practitioners and experts. The direction of a change is based on the body of evidence; however, the magnitude of the impact is our subjective judgment based on the same evidence. Perhaps most importantly, Table 5.1 leaves out an element—empirical evidence or empirical proof of effect—that some might weigh more heavily than qualitative inferences.

Also, as already noted, any number of weighting schemes could be applied that would change a naïve interpretation of the number of elements hypothesized to improve under consolidation. But for us, calling out some elements of a case and setting forth subjective magnitudes of a change is a way of sharpening the debate and squeezing the empirical evidence and subjective inferences into metrics through which informed citizens can agree or disagree about the effects of some factor, thereby improving their discourse on future public policy.

CHAPTER SIX

Conclusions

So, putting our analysis and subjective inferences together, where do we come out on the question of whether consolidation of the City of Pittsburgh and Allegheny County has a reasonable probability of improving the region's economic development? We would argue that some positive changes are within grasp. Even if not demonstrable empirically in other settings, key signs point to some version of consolidation as being helpful. First, *improved policy direction and unity of leadership seems within grasp, and our judgment is that this can have a positive, although likely too difficult to measure, effect on economic development.* Second, *improved coordination and sharpening of economic-development initiatives seems within grasp, and our judgment is that this would have a positive, although again likely too difficult to measure empirically, effect on economic development.*

These conclusions come with two important caveats.

First, any such economic-development gains will require *enhanced coordination and collaboration with the private sector.* The consolidated entity still will have to deal with the need to rationalize the myriad of economic-development efforts under way within the region, including the worthy public-private partnerships and the perception of a bewildering number of programs and agencies that seem to have some responsibility for the economic well-being of the region. This is especially so as the community receives increasing evidence that rapid response—whether to outsiders or insiders—is an unmistakable element of success in economic development.

Second, it seems to us inescapable that *fragmented regulatory processes and intergovernmental competition will remain drags on regional economic development* if the consolidation scheme involves only the city and county. We would argue that consolidation of the city and the county likely is a worthwhile first step, but we recognize that, given the financial and political effort involved to achieve any consolidation, many would argue that consolidation of only the city and county sets the bar too low when assessing the overall returns.

Interview Protocol

(Introduction: About RAND, study purpose, our research question, human-subject policy, and information-disclosure statement.)

1. How do you measure the success of the economic growth and development of your region?

   1a. Why is that [are these] an appropriate measure(s) for your region?

   1b. Should other regions measure the success of their regional economic development this way or are these unique to your region?

2. How has your region been performing against those measures? *[For the past five to 10 years]*.

3. What are the top three barriers preventing your region from performing even better against these measures?

4. What are the top three action items you would recommend or have recommended that should be undertaken to improve the economic development of your region?

5. Are the responsibilities for encouraging and supporting regional economic development in your area consolidated in one or two governments or support groups *[e.g., a chamber of commerce or a nonprofit organization formed to promote the region]* or fragmented across many governments and booster groups?

   5a. *[If consolidated]* Has consolidation helped foster regional economic growth and development? If yes, how? If no, why not?

   5b. *[If not consolidated]* Has fragmentation helped foster regional economic growth and development? If yes, how? If no, why is that?

6. Is unity of leadership or lack thereof an important factor in the success or failure of economic-development efforts in your region?

7. [Describe *hassle factor* as too many agencies exercising some kind of approval over doing business in the region.] Does the hassle factor exist in your region?

   7a. If so, in what way? How has your region worked to ease the hassle factor for businesses?

   7b. If not, why not? How has the region eliminated the hassle factor for businesses?

8. What regions compete against you for new jobs and new firms? What makes these regions most effective when they compete against you?

8a. Does the form of regional government of these areas affect their competitiveness? If so, how?

9. Is there anything about regional economic development or city-county consolidation that we haven't discussed?

Thank you very much.

References

Adams, Robert F., "On the Variation in the Consumption of Public Services," *Review of Economics and Statistics*, Vol. 47, No. 4, November 1965, pp. 400–405.

Brookings Institution, *Back to Prosperity: A Competitive Agenda for Renewing Pennsylvania*, Washington, D.C.: Brookings Institution Center on Urban and Metropolitan Policy, 2003. As of February 29, 2008: http://www.brookings.edu/reports/2003/12metropolitanpolicy_pennsylvania.aspx

Carr, Jered B., Sang-Seok Bae, and Wenjue Lu, "City-County Government and Promises of Economic Development: A Tale of Two Cities," *State and Local Government Review*, Vol. 38, No. 3, 2006, pp. 259–269.

Carr, Jered B., and Richard C. Feiock, "Metropolitan Government and Economic Development," *Urban Affairs Review*, Vol. 34, No. 3, January 1999, pp. 476–488.

———, "Who Becomes Involved in City-County Consolidation? Findings from County Officials in 25 Communities," *State and Local Government Review*, Vol. 34, No. 2, Spring 2002, pp. 78–94.

———, *City-County Consolidation and Its Alternatives: Reshaping the Local Government Landscape*, Armonk, N.Y.: M. E. Sharpe, 2004.

Currid, Elizabeth, "How Art and Culture Happen in New York," *Journal of the American Planning Association*, Vol. 73, No. 4, Autumn 2007, pp. 454–468.

Dahl, Robert A., "The City in the Future of Democracy," *American Political Science Review*, Vol. 61, No. 4, December 1967, pp. 953–970.

Dewar, Margaret E., "Why State and Local Economic Development Programs Cause So Little Economic Development," *Economic Development Quarterly*, Vol. 12, No. 1, February 1998, pp. 68–87.

Drier, Peter, John H. Mollenkopf, and Todd Swanstrom, *Place Matters: Metropolitics for the Twenty-First Century*, Lawrence, Kan.: University Press of Kansas, 2001.

Eberts, Randall W., and Timothy J. Gronberg, "Can Competition Among Local Governments Constrain Government Spending?" *Economic Review* (Federal Reserve Bank of Cleveland), Vol. 24, No. 1, Quarter 1 1988, pp. 2–9.

Feiock, Richard C., "The Political Economy of Growth Management," *American Politics Quarterly*, Vol. 22, No. 2, April 1994, pp. 208–220.

———, ed., *Metropolitan Governance: Conflict, Competition, and Cooperation*, Washington, D.C.: Georgetown University Press, 2004.

Feiock, Richard C., and Jered B. Carr, "A Reassessment of City/County Consolidation: Economic Development Impacts," *State and Local Government Review*, Vol. 29, No. 3, Fall 1997, pp. 166–171.

Felbinger, Claire L., "Economic Development or Economic Disaster? Joliet, Illinois," in Richard D. Bingham and John P. Blair, eds., *Urban Economic Development*, Beverly Hills, Calif.: Sage Publications, 1984.

Feulner, Jason, Julien Hautier, and Ben Walsh, *The Future of Government Consolidation in Upstate New York: A Report to Syracuse 20/20*, Syracuse, N.Y.: Syracuse 20/20, June 2005. As of February 29, 2008: http://www.syracuse2020.org/LinkClick.aspx?fileticket=p6gCWKaagAE%3d&tabid=77&mid=406

Foster, Kathryn A., "Exploring the Links Between Political Structure and Metropolitan Growth," *Political Geography*, Vol. 12, No. 6, November 1993, pp. 523–547.

Frisken, Frances, *Governance and Social Well-Being in the Toronto Area: Past Achievements and Future Challenges*, Toronto: Centre for Urban and Community Studies, University of Toronto, 1997.

Hamilton, David K., David Y. Miller, and Jerry Paytas, "Exploring the Horizontal and Vertical Dimensions of the Governing of Metropolitan Regions," *Urban Affairs Review*, Vol. 40, No. 2, November 2004, pp. 147–182

Howell-Moroney, Michael, "The Tiebout Hypothesis 50 Years Later: Lessons and Lingering Challenges for Metropolitan Governance in the 21st Century," *Public Administration Review*, Vol. 68, No. 1, January–February 2008, pp. 97–109.

Isserman, Andrew M., "Interjurisdictional Spillovers, Political Fragmentation and the Level of Local Public Services: A Re-Examination," *Urban Studies*, Vol. 13, No. 1, 1976, pp. 1–12.

Kugler, Alan R., and Mary C. Bula, *Addressing Needed Changes in Pennsylvania's Local Governance*, Erie, Pa.: Economy League, Northwest Division, 1999.

Leland, Suzanne M., and Gary A. Johnson, "Consolidation as a Local Government Reform: Why City-County Consolidation Is an Enduring Issue," in Jered B. Carr and Richard C. Feiock, eds., *City-County Consolidation and Its Alternatives: Reshaping the Local Government Landscape*, Armonk, N.Y.: M. E. Sharpe, 2004, pp. 25–38.

Leland, Suzanne M., and Kurt M. Thurmaier, eds., *Case Studies of City-County Consolidation: Reshaping the Local Government Landscape*, Armonk, N.Y.: M. E. Sharpe, 2004.

———, "When Efficiency Is Unbelievable: Normative Lessons from 30 Years of City-County Consolidations," *Public Administration Review*, Vol. 65, No. 4, 2005, pp. 475–489.

Lembeck, Stanford M., Tim W. Kelsey, and George W. Fasic, *Measuring the Effectiveness of Comprehensive Planning and Land Use Regulation in Pennsylvania*, Harrisburg, Pa.: Center for Rural Pennsylvania, 2001.

Lind, Michael, "A Horde of Lilliputian Governments," *New Leader*, Vol. 80, No. 8, May 5, 1997, pp. 6–7.

McCarthy, Kevin F., *An Economic Development Architecture for New Orleans*, Santa Monica, Calif.: RAND Corporation, TR-547-HI, 2008. As of March 3, 2008:
http://www.rand.org/pubs/technical_reports/TR547/

Miller, Harold D., "Pittsburgh's Future: Making Southwestern Pennsylvania One of the World's Greatest Regions," undated blog homepage. As of February 29, 2008:
http://pittsburghfuture.blogspot.com

———, "The Persistent Myth About Per Capita Income Growth in Pittsburgh," *Pittsburgh's Future: Making Southwestern Pennsylvania One of the World's Greatest Regions*, November 6, 2007. As of February 29, 2008:
http://pittsburghfuture.blogspot.com/2007/11/persistent-myth-about-per-capita-income.html

NACo—*see* National Association of Counties.

National Association of Counties, "City-County Consolidation Proposals: 1805–Present," undated list. As of February 29, 2008:
http://www.naco.org/Content/NavigationMenu/About_Counties/Data_and_Demographics/City_CountyConsolidationProposals.pdf

Nelson, Arthur C., and Kathryn A. Foster, "Metropolitan Governance Structure and Income Growth," *Journal of Urban Affairs*, Vol. 21, No. 3, 1999, pp. 309–324.

Nelson, Michael A., "An Empirical Analysis of State and Local Tax Structure in the Context of the Leviathan Model of Government," *Public Choice*, Vol. 49, No. 3, January 1986, pp. 283–294.

———, "Searching for Leviathan: Comment and Extension," *American Economic Review*, Vol. 77, No. 1, March 1987, pp. 198–204.

Orfield, Myron, *American Metropolitics: The New Suburban Reality*, Washington, D.C.: Brookings Institution Press, 2002.

Pineda, Chris, *City-County Consolidation and Diseconomies of Scale: Summary of Selected Literature*, Cambridge, Mass.: Ash Institute for Democratic Governance and Innovation, October 2005. As of March 3, 2008:
http://www.innovations.harvard.edu/showdoc.html?id=9331

Pittsburgh's Future, undated homepage. As of February 29, 2008:
http://www.pittsburghfuture.com

PittsburghToday, undated homepage. As of February 29, 2008:
http://www.pittsburghtoday.org

Rosenbaum, Walter A., and Gladys M. Kammerer, *Against Long Odds: The Theory and Practice of Successful Governmental Consolidation*, Beverly Hills, Calif.: Sage Publications, 1974.

Rusk, David, *Cities Without Suburbs*, Washington, D.C.: Woodrow Wilson Center Press, 1993.

Savageau, David, *Retirement Places Rated: What You Need to Know to Plan the Retirement You Deserve*, 7th ed., Hoboken, N.J.: Wiley, 2007.

Savitch, H. V., and Ronald K. Vogel, *Is Louisville Dying? If So, Is Merger the Cure?* manuscript submitted to Darryl Owens, C District Fiscal Court of Jefferson County, Ky., March 22, 1999.

———, "Louisville/Jefferson County, Kentucky: Merger in Louisville-Jefferson County," in Suzanne M. Leland and Kurt M. Thurmaier, eds., *Case Studies of City-County Consolidation: Reshaping the Local Government Landscape*, Armonk, N.Y.: M. E. Sharpe, 2004, pp. 272–290.

Schneider, Mark, "Intercity Competition and the Size of the Local Public Work Force," *Public Choice*, Vol. 63, No. 3, December 1989, pp. 253–265.

Sjoquist, David L., "The Effect of the Number of Local Governments on Central City Expenditures," *National Tax Journal*, Vol. 35, No. 1, March 1982, pp. 79–88.

Sleeper, Sally, Henry H. Willis, Eric Landree, and Beth Grill, *Measuring and Understanding Economic Interdependence in Allegheny County*, Santa Monica, Calif.: RAND Corporation, TR-200-HE, 2004. As of February 29, 2008:
http://www.rand.org/pubs/technical_reports/TR200/

Sleeper, Sally, Henry H. Willis, Stephen Rattien, and Adrienn Lanczos, *A Research Agenda for Assessing the Impact of Fragmented Governance on Southwestern Pennsylvania*, Santa Monica, Calif.: RAND Corporation, TR-139-HE, 2004. As of February 29, 2008:
http://www.rand.org/pubs/technical_reports/TR139/

Sperling, Bert, and Peter J. Sander, *Cities Ranked and Rated: More Than 400 Metropolitan Areas Evaluated in the U.S. and Canada*, 2nd ed., Hoboken, N.J.: Wiley, 2007.

Stephens, G. Ross, and Nelson Wikstrom, *Metropolitan Government and Governance: Theoretical Perspectives, Empirical Analysis, and the Future*, New York: Oxford University Press, 2000.

Tiebout, Charles M., "A Pure Theory of Local Expenditures," *Journal of Political Economy*, Vol. 64, No. 5, October 1956, pp. 416–424.

U.S. Census Bureau, "State and County QuickFacts," undated Web page. As of February 29, 2008:
http://quickfacts.census.gov/qfd/

Wolfson, Joanne, and Frances Frisken, "Local Response to the Global Challenge: Comparing Local Economic Development Policies in a Regional Context," *Journal of Urban Affairs*, Vol. 22, No. 4, 2000, pp. 361–384.